1 MONTH OF FREE READING

at

www.ForgottenBooks.com

By purchasing this book you are eligible for one month membership to ForgottenBooks.com, giving you unlimited access to our entire collection of over 1,000,000 titles via our web site and mobile apps.

To claim your free month visit:

www.forgottenbooks.com/free176996

* Offer is valid for 45 days from date of purchase. Terms and conditions apply.

ISBN 978-0-483-98501-8
PIBN 10176996

This book is a reproduction of an important historical work. Forgotten Books uses
state-of-the-art technology to digitally reconstruct the work, preserving the original format
whilst repairing imperfections present in the aged copy. In rare cases, an imperfection in
the original, such as a blemish or missing page, may be replicated in our edition. We do,
however, repair the vast majority of imperfections successfully; any imperfections that
remain are intentionally left to preserve the state of such historical works.

Forgotten Books is a registered trademark of FB &c Ltd.
Copyright © 2018 FB &c Ltd.
FB &c Ltd, Dalton House, 60 Windsor Avenue, London, SW19 2RR.
Company number 08720141. Registered in England and Wales.

For support please visit www.forgottenbooks.com

THE
Christian Visitor,
ON THE
OLD TESTAMENT:

GENESIS TO JOB.

WHEN THE EAR HEARD ME, THEN IT BLESSED ME; AND WHEN THE EYE SAW ME, IT GAVE WITNESS TO ME:

BECAUSE I DELIVERED THE POOR THAT CRIED, AND THE FATHERLESS, AND HIM THAT HAD NONE TO HELP HIM.

THE BLESSING OF HIM THAT WAS READY TO PERISH CAME UPON ME; AND I CAUSED THE WIDOW'S HEART TO SING FOR JOY.

JOB xxix. 11—13.

THE THE CHRISTIAN VISITOR:

OR, SELECT PORTIONS

OF

The Old Testament:

GENESIS TO JOB.

WITH

EXPOSITIONS AND PRAYERS.

DESIGNED

TO ASSIST THE FRIENDS OF THE SICK AND AFFLICTED.

BY THE REV. WILLIAM JOWETT, M.A.

LATE FELLOW OF ST JOHN'S COLLEGE, CAMBRIDGE.

SECOND EDITION

LONDON:
SEELEY, BURNSIDE, AND SEELEY, FLEET STREET.

—

MDCCCXLVI

LONDON :

PRINTED BY WILLIAM WATTS,
Crown Court, Temple Bar.

PREFACE.

In pursuing the plan of "The Christian Visitor," the Author here enters upon the Books of the Old Testament. The present Volume consists of Selections from the Historical part of it.

The choice of Scripture Passages has been directed by the general intention of the work; which is, to give Evangelical Instruction and Consolation to Afflicted Persons, more especially among the Poor; but in a style adapted equally to all classes of Society.

The earlier Selections from the Book of Genesis are particularly designed to exhibit the great leading doctrines of Man's Ruin by the Fall, and his Recovery by Christ. Six of these Portions (as also No. 22.) are taken from the "Scripture Readings:"

PREFACE.

which work is now out of print, being superseded by the present Series.

It may be expedient to repeat a remark made in the former Volumes; that whenever, in attending the Sick, an entire Portion shall be found too long, a single paragraph or two may suffice at one reading. For example, the one entitled "Review of Life" (page 129) would easily furnish materials for profitable conversation during two or three visits.

The Author humbly commends the Work to Him, whose Sacred Word is here expounded, and whose Blessing is continually implored in the Prayers which accompany the Expositions. May our Saviour, who came "to preach the Gospel to the Poor," graciously render this small Volume a means of Instruction to the Ignorant; of Edification to the Devout; and of Consolation and Encouragement to many Afflicted Servants of God!

CONTENTS.

	Page
PREFACE	iii. iv.
1. The Image of God; Genesis i. 26.	1
2. The Entrance of Sin into the World; Genesis iii 1—13.	6
3. The Same, continued	11
4. The Curse and the Promise; Genesis iii. 14—24.	15
5. The Same, continued	19
6. Labour and Sorrow, our portion here: Comfort, only in Christ; Genesis iii. 16—19.	23
7. Death, the end of all below: Life Eternal, through Christ; Genesis iii. 19.	27
8. Cain and Abel; Genesis iv. 3—15.	31
9. The Flood; Genesis vi. 5—8.	37
10. Abraham offering up Isaac; Genesis xxii. 1—12.	42
11. Jacob's Ladder; Genesis xxviii. 10—22.	49
12. Joseph and his Brethren; Genesis xlv. 1—8.	55
13. A Father's Blessing; Genesis xlviii. 14—16.	60
14. The Last Farewell; Genesis xlix. 33.	65
15. The Passover; Exodus xii. 3—14. and 21—30.	72
16. The Pillar of a Cloud and of Fire; Exodus xiii. 21, 22	80
17. The Manna; Exodus xvi. 11—30.	85
18. Water from the Rock; Exodus xvii 1—7.	91
19. The Law: The First Table; Exodus xx 1—11	97

CONTENTS.

		Page
20.	The Law: the Second Table; Exodus xx. 12—17.	107
21.	The Law, and the Gospel; Exodus xx. 18—21.	114
22.	The Fiery Serpents; Numbers xxi. 5—9.	120
23.	This Great Wilderness; Deuteronomy ii. 7	124
24.	Review of Life; Deuteronomy viii. 2—5.	129
25.	The Character of Joshua; Joshua i. 1—9.	136
26.	The Cities of Refuge; Joshua xx. 1—6.	143
27.	Samuel, a Pattern to the Young; 1 Samuel iii. 1—10.	150
28.	David's Sin and Pardon; 2 Samuel xii. 1—14.	155
29.	Death of an Infant; 2 Samuel xii. 18—23.	163
30.	Dangerous Sickness of a Young Person; 2 Samuel xii. 22.	169
31.	Solomon praying for Wisdom; 1 Kings iii. 5—15.	175
32.	Elijah and the Widow; 1 Kings xvii. 8—16.	182
33.	The Widow's Son; 1 Kings xvii. 17—24.	186
34.	Heartiness in serving God; 2 Chronicles xxxi. 20, 21.	190
35.	Hezekiah, after his Sickness; 2 Chronicles xxxii. 24—26.	194
36.	Sorrow for National Sins; Ezra ix. 4—6.	199
37.	The Patience of Job; Job i. 20—22.	204
38.	The Resurrection of the Dead; Job xix. 25—27	208
39.	The Right Spirit for the Afflicted; Job xxxiv. 31, 32.	212
40.	The Humility of Job; Job xi. 3—5. and xiii. 5, 6.	216

THE CHRISTIAN VISITOR.

ON THE OLD TESTAMENT.

I.

THE IMAGE OF GOD.

Genesis i. 26.

And God said, Let us make man in our image, after our likeness.

In the beginning, when God created Adam and Eve, and placed them in Paradise, he created them wise and holy. They were made after the image of God. He pronounced them, and all his works, to be "very good."

But our parents forfeited their happy state, by breaking the commandment of God. Thus they, and all their posterity, lost that holy image. "All have sinned, and come short of the glory of God." Folly, and sin, and misery, and death, are now our lot. We inherit them from Adam, as a birth-right.

By this mournful change, we are so far fallen from God, that of ourselves we find it utterly impossible even to understand what is meant by His image. But, for ever blessed be his Name! we have in the Bible an abundantly clear revelation on this subject. Oh may the Spirit of God, then, enlighten our understandings, and enable us to behold His nature, as He has revealed it!

There are three ways, in which we may learn what God is; and what Man at his first creation was.

1. First, the Bible *declares* and *describes* the nature of God's image.

He is perfect in wisdom and in holiness. Read the Ten Commandments, which he hath given us. They are perfect: no man could ever find a fault in them. "The law is holy; and the commandment holy, and just, and good." Examine the precepts of the word of God; especially as they are explained, in their full spiritual sense, in the New Testament. How excellent, how useful, how lovely are they all! Consider the dealings of God with men in his government of the world, as set forth in that true history of families and nations, the Bible. These clearly show his justice and power, his wisdom, and, above all, his goodness.

Here, then, we have a book, that informs us what is the will of God. In that holy book we view his image. Therefore, study the Bible; for it is like God. Its Author is God: it is the copy of his mind. Study it with prayer; and in every page you shall see light, wisdom and holiness beaming forth, as the sun when it shineth in its strength.

2. Then, further, the Lord Jesus Christ, as God incarnate, *displays* the image of God under a human form. His dwelling was among the children of men, as "God manifest in the flesh." "No man

hath seen God at any time : the only-begotten Son, which is in the bosom of the Father, he hath declared him." Whoever desires to see the image of God perfectly displayed on earth, should diligently read the four Gospels; at the same time praying for grace to follow the doctrine and example of Christ Jesus. His discourses show how abundantly the Spirit of wisdom dwelt in him. His miracles of mercy show him to have been full of pity and love. In all these, He exhibits to our admiring hearts the very image of God. He is " full of grace and truth."

But chiefly, Christ's dying on the cross for our salvation is such a wonder of mercy, that in this, more than any thing else, we behold the image of God. For God is all holiness, all love. And in the crucifixion of Christ, we see how he hated sin—how he loved us! In studying so wonderful a mystery, however, we cannot advance one step, unless we have the light of the Holy Spirit on our hearts.

3. Fully to understand this subject, therefore, let us remember, that the grace of the Holy Ghost *re-produces* the image of God, in fallen Man. We must have the image of God stamped anew upon our own souls by the Holy Spirit.

This is saving knowledge: and it makes all our other knowledge complete. The image of God is known to those only, who are new created unto holiness. To all others it is a hidden mystery: nay, they even account it foolishness. Believers alone are renewed in the image of God. They alone are spiritual; and they alone discern spiritual things.— And this is a knowledge which goes on continually increasing. On earth, believers resemble God very faintly; but they desire to imitate Him more and more closely: and they shall be made perfectly like him hereafter; for they shall see him as he is.

My friend, reflect whether *you* know what is the image of God. Have you truly understood this doctrine; or, at least, do you desire to understand it? Have you any proof that your heart is stamped anew with God's holy image? Do you study his mind and will, in the Bible? Do you pray for light? Do you love to follow the spotless example of our Lord Jesus Christ?

These, my friend, are great questions. Cousider them well, and reflect whether you have been brought back unto God, through Christ, the only living way. Never be satisfied till you find that the image of God, which we all lost in Adam, has been renewed in your soul, through faith in Christ, who is "the second Adam, the Lord from heaven."

PRAYER.

O Lord God, most holy, just, and good: We adore thee for thy great glory, and for all thy mercies and loving-kindnesses to the children of men. But especially we thank thee for having called us unto thee through Jesus the Mediator, in whom alone we have life, and peace, and hope.

O our God, we are not worthy to take thy name

within our lips: and of ourselves we are not able so much as to lift up a thought unto thee. We have lost the image of thy holiness: we have departed far from thee: we are full of sin, and deserve to be cast out of thy sight, O thou who art of purer eyes than to behold iniquity!

Yet dost thou offer us not only pardon and reconciliation and acceptance with thee, through faith in Christ; but when we cry to thee out of the depth of our corruptions, thou promisest also to create in us a clean heart, and to renew a right spirit within us. Be it unto us, O Lord, according to thy word. Let thy Holy Spirit make all things new within us. Give us an understanding to know thee, a will to serve thee, and a heart to love thee, and to delight in thee. Enable us to put off the old man, which is corrupt; and to put on the new man, which is created in righteousness and true holiness.

Grant to us, we beseech thee, grace to have our conversation such as becometh saints, so that men may see that we are no longer darkness, but now are we light in the Lord. Bring all mankind, and especially our friends and relatives, to the saving knowledge of Christ Jesus. Recover the wanderers: raise the fallen: pity and save the lost.

O Lord, keep us by thy mighty power, faithful even unto death: and then exalt us to thine own right hand, that we may be satisfied with thy likeness, and rest from all our labours in glory everlasting, through Jesus Christ our Saviour and Redeemer. Amen.

II.

THE ENTRANCE OF SIN INTO THE WORLD.

Genesis iii. 1—13.

Now the serpent was more subtle than any beast of the field which the Lord God had made. And he said unto the woman, Yea, hath God said, Ye shall not eat of every tree of the garden?

And the woman said unto the serpent, We may eat of the fruit of the trees of the garden:

But of the fruit of the tree which is in the midst of the garden, God hath said, Ye shall not eat of it, neither shall ye touch it, lest ye die

And the serpent said unto the woman, Ye shall not surely die:

For God doth know, that in the day ye eat thereof, then your eyes shall be opened, and ye shall be as gods, knowing good and evil.

And when the woman saw that the tree was good for food, and that it was pleasant to the eyes, and a tree to be desired to make one wise, she took of the fruit thereof, and did eat; and gave also unto her husband with her; and he did eat.

And the eyes of them both were opened, and they knew that they were naked; and they sewed fig-leaves together, and made themselves aprons.

And they heard the voice of the Lord God walking in the garden in the cool of the day: and Adam and his wife hid themselves from the presence of the Lord God, amongst the trees of the garden.

And the Lord God called unto Adam, and said unto him, Where art thou?

And he said, I heard thy voice in the garden; and I was afraid, because I was naked; and I hid myself.

And he said, Who told thee that thou wast naked? hast thou eaten of the tree, whereof I commanded thee that thou shouldest not eat?

And the man said, The woman whom thou gavest to be with me, she gave me of the tree, and I did eat.

GENESIS III. 1—13.

And the Lord God said unto the woman, What is this that thou hast done? And the woman said, The serpent beguiled me, and I did eat.

EVERY body sees that there is much sin in the world. The Bible is the only book which tells us how it entered.

Our first parents, Adam and Eve, were created by God in his own image; that is, they were perfectly holy, just, and good. They knew God, and loved him. But Satan, the author of all evil, the enemy of God and man, tempted them; and our parents willingly yielded to the temptation. Thus they fell from their happy state of innocence, having lost the image of God. Their children, and children's children, were born in sin: for, " Who can bring a clean thing out of an unclean? Not one." Like David, every one of us must confess, " Behold, I was shapen in iniquity, and in sin did my mother conceive me."

We inherit the various marks of sin in Adam and Eve so exactly, that it will be well to notice them, one by one. And while we do this, may the Holy Spirit deeply convince us of our sinful state!

1. The first thing to be noticed, is, that Eve allowed herself to talk with the serpent. Sin is very deceitful at first: it comes in a pleasant way. We ought to be on our guard, and not listen for a moment to the tempter. Never parley with sin. Never listen to flatterers. They often force themselves upon us: but we ought to tear ourselves away from their company.

2. The next thing to be noticed, is, Eve's curiosity in gazing at the tree which she was forbidden to eat of. So do we very often gaze on forbidden objects. We think we will only just look at them. But when we have allowed ourselves to look, we soon begin to long after them; and then Satan has gained his first advantage over us. A wandering eye may lead to the very worst sins.

3. Eve seems also to have been tempted by her fancy. She "saw that the tree was good for food." She thought so, as she looked at it. So, when we first indulge in forbidden things, their taste seems very sweet; and, for a time, sweeter and sweeter. But, at the last, sin bites like a serpent, and stings like an adder.

4. Eve saw that this was a tree to be desired to make one wise. She wished to be wiser than God intended her to be. This, again, is a very common temptation.—Many young persons wish to read books which they ought not. And grown-up persons are apt to meddle with things that are too high for them. "Vain man would be wise:" and he would be wise in his own way; not by learning from God.

5. Satan said to our first parents, "Ye shall be as gods:" and Eve was gratified by the proud thought. This is just what men wish to be. They long to be independent; to follow their own inclination; to go into the world as their own masters; to have nobody to keep them in. Especially, they cannot bear to have God for their

Master. They will not be hindered by conscience. They set themselves up as wiser than the Bible. They get to dispute about the Bible, and even against it. "Now," they say, "we will be as gods." But then it is, that the devil has gained a great victory over them. Then it is that they become proud, headstrong, and blasphemous.

6. Moreover, Satan told our first parents, "Ye shall not surely die:" and they believed him, rather than God.—Which was right? In every age, the dying and the dead tell us, by millions, that God was true, and Satan false. The world is a grave, continually opening to receive the dead. Still men go on in sin, believing the devil rather than God. They cannot, indeed, now say, "We shall not die;" but they say, "We shall not die soon." Or else they say, "When we die, we shall not go to hell; —there is no such place." The devil wishes sinners to believe that there is no hell. Thus it is that multitudes travel on, passing through the first death to the second death; still believing Satan, and saying, "It shall be well with us in the end." But, at length, "in hell they lift up their eyes, being in torments."

7. Another very common sin is, having hard thoughts of God. Satan said to Eve: "God doth know, that in the day ye eat thereof, ye shall be as gods." As much as to say, "God has used you ill, in forbidding you this tree." And Eve fell in with this evil thought. In the same way many people complain, "The laws of God are very hard;

they are only made to keep me from pleasure." How soon do young persons begin to say, " I wish my parents, or my master, were not so strict : they are keeping me from my rights." This spirit is really the same as rebelling against God. But, alas! we are all continually thinking that God deals hardly by us. There is scarcely any sin so common as impatience: yet it is a sin by which we directly fly in the face of God. Whenever we are impatient, we, in reality, quarrel with what God appoints.

We will consider the other kinds of temptation and sin another time: these are quite enough to meditate upon, for the present. May the Lord humble us by his Spirit; and lead us to bow down before him, crying for mercy! For the sake of his dear Son, Jesus Christ, he is ready to pardon all our sins, though they are more in number than the hairs of our head. Though we are born in sin, yet, by his Holy Spirit, our souls may be born again. Oh, may that Spirit be given to us: so shall we abhor ourselves for our sinfulness, and learn to love the right ways of the Lord!

PRAYER.

O most holy Lord God, who art of purer eyes than to behold iniquity; how vile and abominable must we appear in thy sight! For thou hast known all the thoughts of our hearts, and all our wanderings, from our childhood and youth upward, even unto this day. We were born in sin, and in sin have we lived. Gracious Father, hide thy face from our sins, and blot out all our iniquities. Renew and sanctify our souls; write thy laws in our hearts; and let thy Holy Spirit dwell and rule within us continually. And grant us thy continual grace, that, being renewed in the spirit of our mind, we may serve thee in newness of life; and may love, honour and obey thee, in all our ways, for thy dear Son's sake, Jesus Christ our Lord. Amen.

III.

THE ENTRANCE OF SIN INTO THE WORLD.
(Continued.)

Genesis iii. 1—13. (See page 6.)

We have not yet described all the different kinds of sin, wherein we follow the example of our first parents. It is a very painful thing to meditate upon our own vileness; but we had better know the worst of ourselves, that so we may be led to seek for pardon and reconciliation with God, through Christ's atoning blood.

8. The next thing we observe then, is, How one sinner tempts others to sin. " Eve took of the fruit, and gave unto her husband with her, and he did eat." Alas! many can say, " I never knew of this sin, or that sin, till I was told of it by others." Those whom we keep company with—aye, those that we love the most—may be our worst enemies: for surely no enemy is so much to be

feared, as he who tempts us to sin. Thus it was, alas! that Eve helped forward the ruin of Adam.

9. But, in the next place, it is mournful to see how Adam was over-persuaded by his wife. He ought to have reproved her. He ought to have prayed to God to pardon and restore her: instead of which, he falls into the very same sin.

10. And now we come to notice the worst mark of all;—and yet it is the least regarded by sinners themselves. It is, the sin of endeavouring to hide ourselves from God; shunning the presence of the ever-blessed God! When Adam and his wife heard the voice of the Lord God walking in the garden, they hid themselves from the presence of the Lord God, among the trees of the garden. They no longer loved God: they dreaded him, and endeavoured to fly from him.—And such, alas! is the real state of all sinners. The presence of God is not desired by them; his name is painful to them; his worship is wearisome. They do not pray to him in secret. They do not love his holy word. They make no hearty preparation for meeting him at the Judgment-day. They take no delight in thinking of the holiness and happiness of heaven. They even try *not* to think of God, and are offended with those who speak to them about Religion. What good men love, *they* hate; namely, Communion with God. This hatred of communion with God is their greatest sin: it is also their greatest misery. But sinners are so far gone in sin, that they do not know how great a misery this

is. God is love, and in his presence is fulness of joy: what wretchedness, then, must we suffer, if we fly from him!

11. Another very common thing with sinners is, Making excuses, and throwing the blame on others. When Adam and Eve are called to give account of themselves, Adam throws the blame on his wife, and partly on God himself: and then Eve throws the blame on the serpent. But in vain does any sinner ask of God, "Why hast thou made me thus?"—or, "Why was I born into a world of sin?"—or, "Why do I inherit a body of sin and death?" In vain do sinners reproach one another. In vain do they curse the devil for tempting and destroying them. Oh, what a dreadful place must hell be, where lost souls and devils are for ever cursing God and one another, yet find no rest from their torments! Others, it is true, are to blame, together with each sinner. Tempters, especially, are a most cruel race: but every lost soul shall bear his own burden. " The soul that sinneth, it shall die."

O sinner! dost thou not behold many of these deadly marks of sin in thyself? Search, and examine. Be willing to know the worst: then thou wilt desire the salvation that is in Christ Jesus. For, blessed be God! we are not *in* hell, though we deserve hell. God accuses us; conscience condemns us; and the devil desires to have us: but the voice of mercy cries, " Deliver him from going down to the pit: I have found a ransom." That ransom is Christ. " As in Adam all die, even so in Christ shall all be made alive." " Whosoever believeth in Him, shall not perish, but have everlasting life." Look, then, at all these evidences of sin in yourself, one by one: but look, also, on the wounds of your bleeding Saviour. Fly to Him, in faith; remembering this declaration in the word of God—" The blood of Jesus Christ, his Son, cleanseth us from all sin."

PRAYER.

O Lord, what shall we say unto thee, or what shall we speak, or how shall we clear ourselves, when we remember how grievously we have sinned against thee? Suffer us not to think of hiding ourselves from thy sight: for thine eye hath been over us continually, and thou knowest us far better than we know ourselves. But bring us to a godly repentance, and hatred of sin: pour upon us the Spirit of grace and of supplications: cause us to look upon Him whom we have pierced, and may we loathe ourselves at the remembrance of all our transgressions. And oh, lead us to that Fountain which is opened for sin and for uncleanness, that in it we may wash and be clean! Let the blood of Jesus Christ, thy Son, cleanse us from all sin! See if there be any wicked way in us, and lead us in the way everlasting, for Jesus Christ's sake. Amen.

IV.

THE CURSE AND THE PROMISE.

Genesis iii. 14—24

And the Lord God said unto the serpent, Because thou hast done this, thou art cursed above all cattle, and above every beast of the field: upon thy belly shalt thou go, and dust shalt thou eat all the days of thy life:

And I will put enmity between thee and the woman, and between thy seed and her seed: it shall bruise thy head, and thou shalt bruise his heel.

Unto the woman he said, I will greatly multiply thy sorrow and thy conception: in sorrow thou shalt bring forth children; and thy desire shall be to thy husband, and he shall rule over thee.

And unto Adam he said, Because thou hast hearkened unto the voice of thy wife, and hast eaten of the tree, of which I commanded thee, saying, Thou shalt not eat of it: cursed is the ground for thy sake; in sorrow shalt thou eat of it all the days of thy life:

Thorns also and thistles shall it bring forth to thee; and thou shalt eat the herb of the field;

In the sweat of thy face shalt thou eat bread, till thou return unto the ground; for out of it wast thou taken: for dust thou art, and unto dust shalt thou return.

And Adam called his wife's name Eve; because she was the mother of all living.

Unto Adam also and to his wife did the Lord God make coats of skins, and clothed them.

And the Lord God said, Behold, the man is become as one of us, to know good and evil: and now, lest he put forth his hand, and take also of the tree of life, and eat, and live for ever;

Therefore the Lord God sent him forth from the garden of Eden, to till the ground from whence he was taken.

So he drove out the man: and he placed, at the east of the garden of Eden, cherubims, and a flaming sword which turned every way, to keep the way of the tree of life.

WHEN Adam and Eve fell, the serpent, who had deceived them, was the first to receive sentence of condemnation. Very dreadful was the curse pronounced upon Satan by God, for having done this wicked thing, bringing sin and death into the world. The wrath of God is upon the devil and his angels eternally. But in pronouncing the curse, God united with it a remarkable promise of redemption to man.

1. When we consider the condemnation of that old serpent, the devil, we shall find, from Scripture, that it is dreadful, beyond all that we can conceive: he is condemned to the lowest hell. Our Saviour speaks of "everlasting fire, prepared for the devil and his angels."

In allusion to the same wretched beings, St. Jude, in his Epistle, speaks of "the angels which kept not their first estate, but left their own habitation:" and he adds, that God hath "reserved them in everlasting chains, under darkness, to the Judgment of the Great Day." St. John also describes the manner in which "an angel came down from heaven, having the key of the bottomless pit, and a great chain in his hand;" and how he "laid hold on the dragon, that old serpent, which is the devil, and Satan;" and bound him in hell.

2. But when God pronounced this curse upon Satan, he declared that he would put enmity between Satan and his seed on the one side, and the woman and her Seed on the other side. Here is a

great mystery. It signifies, that Satan and all the children of disobedience, who are children of the devil, will always be fighting against Jesus Christ: for Christ, the Son of the Virgin Mary, is "the Seed of the woman" here meant. And not only against him will they make war, but also against all true disciples of Christ. But then it is also declared, that Christ will gain the victory. I will give you some examples of this.

Cain, the first-born of Adam and Eve, was of that wicked one, the devil. The devil, who was a murderer from the beginning, stirred up the heart of Cain to murder his brother Abel. "And wherefore slew he him? Because his own works were evil, and his brother's righteous." Here was the first instance of Satan's enmity against the children of God. But Abel was exalted to heaven, and is had in everlasting remembrance. Thus was Satan's enmity disappointed; while Cain was driven out as a vagabond, with a mark set upon him.

Just before the Flood, the world had fallen into a most wicked state. "The earth was corrupt before God, and the earth was filled with violence." God therefore punished the world of the ungodly, by the waters of a flood. Yet still, Satan's object was defeated: the race of man was not lost, though contracted to a single family. Noah and his family were saved in the ark.—This ark, moreover, was intended to show forth the Church of Christ; which will always be safe, even when the world comes to the worst.

There are many more things, which we will say another time, on this subject. But let me now ask you one or two questions. Have you ever felt anger and hatred dwelling in your heart? I fear that all of us have sometimes fallen into sinful tempers. But what a dreadful thing this is! It is like carrying a serpent in our bosom: nay, it is really having the devil in our hearts. Have you sometimes been violent or cruel? Have you dealt in blows and cursings? What a mercy it is, that, in our angry moments, we have not gone so far as murder! But, remember, "he that hateth his brother is a murderer." Oh, what a dreadful thing, when, as is sometimes the case, a whole neighbourhood is filled with noise and violence, and there is scarce one righteous family, nay, scarce one righteous man, among them! It is the devil broke loose on earth.

The good Lord forgive us all those sins in which we have been so much like the devil: and may he make us like his own dear Son, whose soul was gentle as a Lamb!

PRAYER.

O most holy God! who can tell what an evil and bitter thing it is to depart from thee; and how dreadful is the portion of those, who are banished from thy presence for ever? Wonderful is thy mercy, that we have not long since been shut up in hell! But since thou hast spared us, oh, let us now make haste to seek and to obtain thy mercy! Take away from us all hardness of heart, all enmity against thee, and all envy, malice, and uncharitableness toward men. Unite us, by a living faith, to Jesus our Saviour. Write upon our hearts the law of love, that we may seek thy face with joy, and delight to do thy holy will, and be continually given to works of kindness and pity. And grant, that having faithfully served thee in thy Church here below, we may dwell before thee for ever in thy Church above, through Jesus Christ our Lord. Amen.

V.

THE CURSE AND THE PROMISE. (*Continued.*)
GENESIS iii. 14—24. (See page 15.)

THE Bible is full of histories, showing how Satan tries to enslave and ruin every man living. But Christ is able to overcome him: and he certainly will overcome at the last. Perhaps you would like that I should point out to you some more of the ways in which Satan has tried for the mastery, and how God has always overcome him.

Pharaoh, king of Egypt, was a cruel oppressor of the children of Israel. He went even so far as to command, that all the male children of the Israelites should be thrown into the river, and drowned. This was, indeed, like a true child of the devil. But God visited the land with dreadful plagues, to punish him and his people. And on the night of the Passover (which we shall read about another time), the angel of the Lord went forth, and destroyed all the first-born in the land of Egypt, both of man and beast. Thus Pharaoh was terrified, and God delivered Israel out of his hand.—Again, the Egyptians were pushed on by Satan once more, and the Lord suffered them to follow his people into the Red Sea; but there he swallowed up Pharaoh, and all his army, in the depths of the sea. Then the Israelites triumphed in Jehovah. And as the Lord conquered Pharoah and all his army, so will Christ conquer the devil and all his angels; and then the redeemed of the Lord will for ever sing the song of Moses and of the Lamb. The glorious theme of that immortal song is, Redemption.

When Jesus Christ, the Son of God, took upon him the form of man, and dwelt on earth, the devil came to tempt him. But Christ overcame his temptations. Satan even dared to quote Scripture, and thus endeavoured to mislead Christ. But Jesus saw through his deep subtlety, and answered him with most suitable passages of Scripture. This shows the great advantage of knowing the Bible well; for with the help of the Bible we shall be able to fight, as our Saviour did, against Satan. And if we know the whole sense of the Bible well, we shall not be easily deceived by false teachers.

It was when the devil had entered into the heart of Judas Iscariot, that Judas proceeded to betray his Master, Jesus Christ. Satan seemed thus to have got a great victory over the Son of God: yet it was by this very way that Jesus conquered Satan. For St. Paul says, that through death Christ destroyed him that had the power of death, even the devil; and delivered them who, through fear of death, were all their life-time subject to bondage.

As soon as there was a Church of Christ established in any place by the faithful preaching of the Gospel, Satan did all he could to overthrow it. For this purpose he stirred up many people to persecute; but they did not prevail. Christ gave his disciples grace to endure all things for the sake of the Gospel. See how he speaks to the persecuted Church of Smyrna: " Fear none of those things which thou shalt suffer: behold, the devil shall cast some of you into prison, that ye may be tried; and ye shall have tribulation ten days. Be thou faithful unto death, and I will give thee a crown of life."

But there is another warfare between Christ and Satan; which all feel in their hearts, when they try to serve God in earnest. Christ says, " Love the ways of Religion:" Satan whispers to us, " Religion is a very melancholy thing." Christ says, " Keep my sayings in your heart:" but the devil comes, and tries to snatch them away. Christ teaches us how to pray: but Satan tries to hinder us from prayer. Now, which of these two shall prevail in your heart—Christ, or the devil?

If you will choose Christ, you will find him the best Master.—Perhaps you say, " But Satan is so busy about my heart: he is too active, and too cunning for me. When I wish to be religious, he turns all my thoughts the wrong way. When I would do good, evil is present with me. When I wish to fly from bad company, they follow after me, and laugh at me. When I am beginning to think of good thoughts, just then bad thoughts come into my mind. What am I to do? How can I conquer this enemy, who is so cunning, and so hard upon me?"

My friend, the answer is very plain. Entreat Christ to be your friend. Let him dwell in your heart by faith. Where Christ reigns, Satan may try to be master, but he never can succeed. Open your heart to Christ in prayer. Tell him all your temptations. Beseech him to cast out Satan, and to take possession of your heart. Satan may torment and trouble your mind: but this is the promise—" Christ will bruise the head of Satan." He will set his foot upon him, and crush him. This he will do, if only you continue praying in the name of Christ:

"For Satan trembles, when he sees
The weakest saint upon his knees."

PRAYER.

O Lord Jesu Christ, who hast overcome death, and brought life and immortality to light through the Gospel; enable us, we beseech thee, faithfully to follow thee, and to fight manfully against the world, the flesh, and the devil. In every time of trial and temptation, be thou our hiding-place and refuge. Suffer not the enemy to prevail, or do us harm. Deliver us from the curse and the dominion of sin, that we may enjoy peace and safety through thee. Speak comfortably to our souls, whenever we mourn before thee with a godly sorrow for sin. Purge our consciences from dead works; and bestow on us the joy of thy salvation, to strengthen us for thy continual service. Guide us in the path of holiness through life; and finally, in the hour of death, and in the Day of Judgment, Good Lord deliver us. Amen.

VI.

LABOUR AND SORROW, OUR PORTION HERE: COMFORT, ONLY IN CHRIST.

Genesis iii. 16—19.

Unto the woman he said, I will greatly multiply thy sorrow and thy conception: in sorrow thou shalt bring forth children; and thy desire shall be to thy husband, and he shall rule over thee.

And unto Adam he said, Because thou hast hearkened unto the voice of thy wife, and hast eaten of the tree, of which I commanded thee, saying, Thou shalt not eat of it: cursed is the ground for thy sake; in sorrow shalt thou eat of it all the days of thy life;

Thorns also, and thistles, shall it bring forth to thee; and thou shalt eat the herb of the field;

In the sweat of thy face shalt thou eat bread, till thou return unto the ground; for out of it wast thou taken: for dust thou art, and unto dust shalt thou return.

WHEN Adam and Eve had sinned against God, the ground was cursed for their sake. The children of men are now born into a world very different from the Paradise in which our first parents were placed. Pain and death were not known there: but when sin entered into the world, the curse immediately followed.

Concerning death, we will speak another time. What we have now to do with, is, the misery of man in this world, and the cure of that misery.

David says, " Behold, I was shapen in iniquity, and in sin did my mother conceive me." This is the consequence of Adam's sin. Therefore, at the time of our birth, we enter the world with cries and tears; and the portion of man, on the earth, is, as Job says, to be of few days, and full of trouble. " Man is born to trouble, as the sparks fly upward."

The earth, you know, brings forth plenty of weeds and thistles, briers and thorns: but to make it fit for sowing corn, men must plough and harrow; they must bear the hardships of winter, and the heat of summer; and thus, by the sweat of their face, they at length " eat bread."

You know, that in great towns and cities also, man's lot is to labour. Men " rise up early, and late take rest, and eat the bread of carefulness;" and some get very little sleep.

The poor often think this very hard. Still, we may be sure of one thing; namely, that riches do not of themselves make a man happy. They afford happiness only when used for God's glory. Perhaps you see a rich man well fed, finely dressed, and riding in a carriage; and you think, because he sits at his ease, and because he does not work with his hands, therefore he is happy. But this is a great mistake. No man can escape the general curse. The rich have many troubles; and those of them that are not pious, are often more tired with not knowing what to do, than the poor are with having too much to do.

Remember that simple prayer, which Jesus Christ has taught us: " Give us this day our daily bread." The Lord hears the young ravens that call upon him: and will he not feed his own children that pray to him?

Contentment is learned only in the school of Christ; for there we learn, that we always suffer less than our sins deserve. And in our Master, Christ Jesus, we have such a picture of " the Holy One of God" suffering for our sins, as should make us ashamed, whenever we murmur.

Men who live without God are always seeking for ease in this world, yet cannot find it. The best way is, to labour on, with our hands, or with our head, or both, to the last. It is better to wear out, than to rust out. Idleness is misery: honest labour is the best for man.

When sickness or grievous calamities come, we ought to say, " This is from the hand of the Lord. The Lord gave, and the Lord hath taken away; blessed be the name of the Lord!"

Every true believer in Christ has a source of solid comfort, which the rest of the world know not of. He knows that his sins are forgiven him, through faith in Christ. Believing his soul to be safe for eternity, he knows he need not fear what his body may suffer in this world.

The great question is, " Have you chosen the

Lord for your portion?" Do you rest in Christ as your Saviour? Do you lament your sins more than your afflictions? Do you find your burdens made lighter by prayer? Does prayer lead you to praise? Do you rejoice in the hope of heaven, where "the wicked cease from troubling, and where the weary are at rest?" Oh, if you knew Christ, and if you really lived on him by faith, no sorrows of this life would ever overwhelm you! You would find that "all things work together for good to them that love God." You would feel that you have, in Christ, a fellow-sufferer. You would read the Gospels with new delight: for there we see how Jesus, "though he was rich, yet for our sakes became poor, that we through his poverty might be rich."

But do not think that your present sufferings can purchase heaven. We can of ourselves deserve nothing but eternal punishment. The impenitent and unbelieving must suffer, both in this world and in the next. Seek, then, for salvation by Christ, as a free gift; and having this, you have all!

PRAYER.

O Lord, thou righteous Judge of all the earth; what miseries hast thou laid upon the children of men, on account of our many transgressions against thee! We have sinned, and done wickedly: but thou continuest holy, O thou worship of Israel! But, as thy justice is, so is thy mercy also toward us, miserable sinners. Thou hast laid help upon

One that is mighty; even on Jesus, our crucified Redeemer, who is able to save to the uttermost all that come unto thee by him.

Oh, suffer us not to perish through our own obstinacy, or unbelief! Incline our hearts to look unto Jesus. Let us never fall into despair, when we behold so dear a ransom paid for our souls, even the precious blood of Jesus. O Lord, let us not sink under the load of our sins; but enable us to cast the heavy burden on Him, who bore our sins in his own body on the tree. Take out from our consciences the sting and the tormenting power of sin, through the grace of Him, who was bruised that we might be healed, and who died that we might live, even Jesus Christ our Lord. Amen.

VII.

DEATH, THE END OF ALL BELOW: LIFE ETERNAL, THROUGH CHRIST.

Genesis iii. 19.

In the sweat of thy face shalt thou eat bread, till thou return unto the ground; for out of it wast thou taken: for dust thou art, and unto dust shalt thou return.

To most men it is very melancholy to think of death. Yet, if we are true Christians, we shall be willing to think of it; and, through the mercy of our Lord Jesus Christ, this mournful subject will be changed into a delightful one. Through him the sting of death is quite taken away, and we may obtain victory over our last enemy.

See how the curse pronounced on Adam has been fulfilled, and is fulfilling, on all the generations of men! Death, like an irresistible king, reigns over us all. He holds in his hand an iron sceptre; and when he smites, none can escape. Alike the rich and the poor, the weak and the strong, infants and grey-headed men, are every moment dropping into the grave. Every one that is born into the world must say with Job, " I know that thou wilt bring me unto death, and to the house appointed for all living."

Nor is it death only that is mournful, but all the way that leads to it. When we are in health and spirits, we think too little of this. But we should reflect on this curse, in all the sicknesses which mankind suffer. Think of the diseases and pains, the sighs, tears, and groans, which keep us company on our road to the grave. Truly, man, in his best estate, is altogether vanity! In the midst of life, we are in death. The healthy and the gay *try not to think* of these things; and they are offended, if spoken to about dying. They do not consider that *their* turn may come very quickly. But wise men will lay this to heart: they will say, " Depart from me, ye sinful pleasures; and let me prepare for death and eternity!"

Would you know what it is that makes death terrible? St. Paul will answer the question. He says, " The sting of death is sin." It was sin that brought death into the world; and it is the remembrance of our sins that makes it terrible to think of dying. Oh, if we could but cast off this burden of sin—could we only be assured that God is our Friend, and heaven our portion after death—who then would fear to die? Instead of cleaving to the world, we should even desire "to depart, and to be with Christ, which is far better." Oh, then, seek to win Christ, and to be found in him! Through faith in his precious blood, be reconciled to God. Mortify all worldly lusts, and live as one that loves the appearing of our Lord Jesus. Then, to *you*, death will no longer be a king of terrors, but a messenger of peace.

When Jesus descended into the grave, he made the dark way safe for all that believe in Him. After three days, he burst the tomb, and rose from the dead. In like manner, at the great Judgment-day, he will call the dead, small and great, to come and stand before him. Those who, at that day, are living on the earth, will be caught up in the air. And all " that are in their graves, shall hear his voice, and shall come forth." Those who, on earth, did not believe in Christ, nor serve him, will then be utterly consumed with terrors: they will be driven into outer darkness, where shall be weeping, and wailing, and gnashing of teeth, for ever. "This is the second death!" This ought to make every sinner tremble. O sinner! take no rest, no sleep —enjoy no pleasure, no company—till thou hast prayed earnestly to Jesus, to deliver thee from the wrath to come! For thy soul's sake, repent, believe, and turn to God. Pray for his Holy Spirit to change thy heart. O sinner! with such an evil heart as thine, thou *canst not* enter into the kingdom of heaven. Pray that it may be made a new heart. No longer remain dead in trespasses and sins, lest the hour of death should find thee unprepared. But cry mightily to God; and remember, that " *now* is the accepted time; *now* is the day of salvation."

But, perhaps, you have begun to believe in the Lord Jesus Christ; and you desire to live and die in his service. If so, let Him be your hope, your joy, your rest. Let not Satan trouble you with the fear of dying. Sometimes you may be low-spirited, and ready to sink. At such moments, let this short sentence comfort your heart, " CHRIST DIED FOR ME."—And when, at last, we come to die, may some kind Christian friend be near at hand, to whisper in our ears these blessed words, " I know that my Redeemer liveth!" " O death, where is thy sting? O grave, where is thy victory? Thanks be to God, who giveth us the victory, through our Lord Jesus Christ!"

PRAYER.

Blessed Jesus, our Lord and our God; our Life, our Hope, our Glory! O fix our hearts on thee, and make them wholly thine! Thou didst pity us, while sinners: thou didst seek us, when wanderers: and thou didst lay down thy life for our sake. God forbid that we should glory, save in the cross of our Lord Jesus Christ!

And now, what shall we render unto the Lord,

for this his unspeakable gift? Lord, we can only offer the sacrifice of a broken heart, which thy word hath said, Thou wilt not despise. We present ourselves unto thee, to be made willing and obedient; an habitation of God, through the Spirit. O accept us, Heavenly Father, in Christ, thy wellbeloved Son! And let the same mind be in us which was also in Him. Fill us with meekness, humility, and love. Incline us to pity all wanderers from thy fold, even all our dying fellow-sinners upon earth. Teach us to seek out sinners, and bring them, by all means, to thee, O gracious Father, that they may be saved.

And, whenever we are tempted aside into forbidden pastures, O speedily cause us to hear and know the voice of Jesus; and incline our hearts to return again to this good Shepherd and Bishop of our souls, to Jesus, our Redeemer and our Lord. Amen.

VIII.

CAIN AND ABEL.

Genesis iv. 3—15.

And in process of time it came to pass, that Cain brought of the fruit of the ground, an offering unto the Lord.

And Abel, he also brought of the firstlings of his flock, and of the fat thereof. And the Lord had respect unto Abel, and to his offering:

But unto Cain, and to his offering, he had no respect. And Cain was very wroth, and his countenance fell.

And the Lord said unto Cain, Why art thou wroth? and why is thy countenance fallen?

If thou doest well, shalt thou not be accepted? and if thou doest not well, sin lieth at the door. And unto thee shall be his desire, and thou shalt rule over him.

And Cain talked with Abel his brother: and it came to pass, when they were in the field, that Cain rose up against Abel his brother, and slew him.

And the Lord said unto Cain, Where is Abel thy brother? And he said, I know not: Am I my brother's keeper?

And he said, What hast thou done? the voice of thy brother's blood crieth unto me from the ground.

And now art thou cursed from the earth, which hath opened her mouth to receive thy brother's blood from thy hand.

When thou tillest the ground, it shall not henceforth yield unto thee her strength; a fugitive and a vagabond shalt thou be in the earth.

And Cain said unto the Lord, My punishment is greater than I can bear.

Behold, thou hast driven me out this day from the face of the earth: and from thy face shall I be hid; and I shall be a fugitive and a vagabond in the earth: and it shall come to pass, that every one that findeth me shall slay me.

And the Lord said unto him, Therefore whosoever slayeth Cain, vengeance shall be taken on him seven-fold. And the Lord set a mark upon Cain, lest any finding him should kill him.

ADAM, having lost the image of God, soon tasted the bitter consequences of sin. His children were born in his image. Cain, the first-born, unrestrained by divine grace, became the persecutor, and even the murderer of his younger brother, the pious Abel.

We have so often heard of Cain, as the first murderer, that many are apt to think murder was his only great crime. But if we look carefully into the case, we shall find that other great sins accompanied this heinous action, and even led the way to it.

May that enlightening Spirit, by whose inspiration the Bible was written, assist us in meditating on this affecting story!

1. The first sin of Cain was, Presumption: he pretended to worship God; but he worshipped in a way of his own choosing. He came, as an innocent man might have done, with simply a thank-offering: while Abel, as a contrite sinner, worshipped according to the will of God, bringing a sacrifice. It is expressly said (Hebrews xi. 4), that "by faith Abel offered unto God a more excellent sacrifice than Cain." Cain brought an offering of the fruit of the ground; but Abel brought of the firstlings of his flock. These were types of the sacrifice of Christ, the promised Redeemer. And the Lord had respect unto Abel, and to his offering; but unto Cain, and to his offering, he had not respect.—The grand thing in Religion is, obedient faith. Abel had this faith: Cain had it not.

Self-will, even in worldly things, is a grievous fault, and leads many a man to ruin: but in religious matters, it is a high crime against God. Few persons think of this. All abhor Cain as a murderer; but very few discern the wickedness of his self-willed worship.

2. A further sin of Cain, was, his spirit of proud Anger against God. God had marked his displeasure against Cain: and Cain acted as if he had a right to be angry with God. When God had not respect to his offering, his countenance fell. Instead

of humbly repenting, he sullenly resented God's frown. Just the same is the temper of self-righteous men, stumbling at Gospel-Truth. Instead of meekly receiving God's mercy through Christ, they are vexed to see that the way of Salvation is so humbling; and they are angry, both with God, and with those who are humble enough to accept his free grace.

3. Hence sprang Cain's enmity against his brother—enmity, that went on to Murder! Abel now became an object of envy and hatred to Cain. The more spiritual and humble godly men are, so much the more persecution may they expect to suffer from wicked and self-righteous men. The fact is plainly laid down in Scripture; "All who will live godly in Christ Jesus, shall suffer persecution:" there never was an exception to this. The first instance was Cain murdering his brother Abel. This is a specimen of what every ungodly man feels, though few *show* all the malice of their hearts against godly men, and against godliness. What an affecting proof, of the natural vileness of our hearts! Think of our hating those who are better than ourselves; yea, hating those who are beloved of God! What a fearful state! "He that hateth his brother is a murderer; and ye know that no murderer hath eternal life abiding in him."

Few suspect how deeply the hatred of holiness is rooted in the natural man. While there is no bright example near us, we think ourselves incapable of envy. But when an unconverted man is reproved, ever so gently, by one of God's faithful servants, a feeling of resentment is soon kindled in his breast.

4. The last thing recorded concerning Cain, after the murder, is, his refusing to repent. When summoned by the voice of God to give account of his horrid crime—when asked, in words which plainly showed that God knew what he had done, " Where is Abel thy brother?"—does he humble himself? No. He pretends that it is no business of his. He answers, "Am I my brother's keeper?" And when condemned and cursed by God himself, he murmurs out, " My punishment is greater than I can bear." In all this, he shows not the slightest mark of godly sorrow. Still less does he show any faith in the promised Redeemer, who pardons even murderers, when they repent, and believe in him. He goes away, a thoroughly wretched and accursed man.—And how does this fugitive and vagabond in the earth employ himself? All that we read concerning the remainder of his days, is, that he went into another country, and was engaged in building cities, and minding worldly things.

What awful lessons are taught by this history! Adam and Eve would now see what it was to have a son " conceived in sin, and shapen in iniquity." We, too, may here learn what it is to be self-willed towards God, and what is the enmity of the carnal heart against him. Here we behold the very picture of a child of the Devil; full of pride, envy, hatred, cruelty, and earthly-minded-ness. Oh, may God deliver us from these awful passions!

Now view the end of righteous Abel. He was barbarously cut off from the land of the living: but he was carried by angels to rest in the bosom of his Heavenly Father. No more does the cruel voice of Cain grate on his ear : he entered at once into a family where all is love. His name stands foremost, in the noble army of martyrs: he first was crowned in the glorious Church above. He has, by his life and death, left us a most precious example of faith in the Redeemer;—a faith, which will be celebrated from generation to generation, world without end.

PRAYER.

O Lord, who hast revealed unto us thy Son Jesus Christ, as the way, the truth, and the life: Help us to come unto thee in prayer and thanksgiving, making mention of His name, even His only. We have no righteousness of our own, wherein to stand before thee : we would come, therefore, pleading the merits of thy dear Son, and clothed with the righteousness which is of God by faith. And when we thus approach thee, in thine own appointed way, grant unto us acceptance, and life eternal, through thy well-beloved Son, Christ Jesus.

When we are called to endure reproach or injury for Christ's sake, give us grace, O Lord, to rejoice in it, and to bear it with all long-suffering and meekness. Strengthen us, that we may with constancy abide in the truth of thy holy Gospel; and maintain it, if needs be, even unto death. O fill us with the Holy Ghost and with faith, that we may glorify Thee both in word and deed, and patiently endure whatsoever may come upon us for the truth's sake.

Lord, restrain the malice and cruelty of those who hate thy cause and thy people. Give peace in our time, O Lord. Graciously protect, deliver, and bless all those who are persecuted for righteousness' sake.

Hear us, O Lord God of our salvation, for the glory of thy Name, through Jesus Christ our Lord. Amen.

IX.

THE FLOOD.

Genesis vi. 5—8.

And God saw that the wickedness of man was great in the earth, and that every imagination of the thoughts of his heart was only evil continually.

And it repented the Lord that he had made man on the earth, and it grieved him at his heart.

And the Lord said, I will destroy man, whom I have created, from the face of the earth; both man, and beast, and the creeping thing, and the fowls of the air: for it repenteth me that I have made them.

But Noah found grace in the eyes of the Lord.

The world had been created, and inhabited by mankind for more than fifteen hundred years, when this awful judgment was executed. God, in anger, sent a flood of waters to destroy the whole race of men, one family alone excepted! Let us meditate on this event, praying that the Spirit of God would fill us with humble and holy fear.

1. The reason of this judgment is here given. It was because "God saw that the wickedness of man was great in the earth." "All flesh had corrupted his way upon the earth." "The earth was filled with violence."

Nor was this all. Not only had sin risen to its highest pitch, but sinners remained impenitent, and were hardened in their guilt. Enoch, that holy man, who "walked with God," had prophesied that judgments were coming: but his warning was slighted; or rather, he was answered with hard speeches, by the scoffers and mockers of that day. During a hundred and twenty years, God showed the greatest long-suffering, warning them and waiting to be gracious, if they would turn and repent. Noah was a preacher of righteousness through all that long season of forbearance. He told them of God's threatenings: and he preached not by words only, but by actions also, building his ark from day to day in the sight of God's enemies; nay, most probably, with the actual help of *their* hands, while they received wages for their work. They built the ark, and were paid for it: but they were not saved by it: it floated on the mighty flood of waters, a monument of their guilt. Thus, besides all their other sins, they were guilty of unbelief: they turned a deaf ear to the warnings of

God, and shut their eyes to the light of Noah's holy example.

Think, my friend—What *can* be done for sinners, such as these? And yet, think again—Are there none like them, in our day? Are there none who corrupt themselves, walking after their own lusts? Are there none, among us, making a jest of Religion? Are there none who utter hard speeches against the godly? Are there none who deny the Bible, and laugh at the threatened judgments of God? Are there none who trample under foot the blood of Jesus, and resist his Holy Spirit?

Alas! there are, we fear, many such: very many, indeed, are they that walk in the broad road that leadeth to destruction! Are *we* come out of it?

2. Now observe, that, when the forbearance of God is worn out by the sin and obstinacy of the wicked, then judgment must and will come on them. " Though hand join in hand, yet the wicked shall not be unpunished." " He that, being often reproved, hardeneth his neck, shall suddenly be cut off, and that without remedy." As surely as the flood came and swept away the ungodly, so surely shall the dreadful Day of Judgment come; when " the wicked shall be turned into hell, and all the nations that forget God."

Perhaps you say—" I do not see the truth of this. Year after year, and generation after generation, I find that all things continue just as they used to be. We cannot, indeed, help dying: but *that*, I hope, is the worst: for I cannot by any means bring myself to believe in the doctrine of hell-torments."

Such is the way, in which many persons talk and think. The reason is, they do not like to be disturbed in their sins. But will our not feeling, or our not believing, change the purpose of God? Certainly not. Sinners *must* perish, whether they believe it or not.

Sinners fill up their time with business and pleasure, in order to keep death and judgment out of their thoughts. Thus it was in the days of Noah: " they were eating and drinking, marrying and giving in marriage, until the day that Noah entered into the ark; and knew not, until the flood came and took them all away." They " knew not:" that is, they believed not, and therefore made no sort of preparation for their last hour.

3. " But Noah found grace in the eyes of the Lord." He was a holy man; having been made holy and separate from sinners by the grace of God. It was God who made him to differ from others. " He walked with God." He believed the word of God: he feared the coming judgment: and he obeyed the command to build an ark for the saving of his house. In all this he was a pattern to us, and to all mankind, even to the latest generation.

The preservation of Noah in the ark is a figure of our salvation by Christ Jesus. Christ is our only Ark: salvation by faith in Him we must all accept, or we must perish. Think, O sinner, of the wrath of God which lieth on thee! Thou canst not endure that wrath: thy sins are as a burden too heavy for thee to bear! Then, behold this burden borne by Christ in his own body on the cross—behold thy punishment laid on him—thy debt paid by his free grace—thy salvation bought with the precious blood of Jesus, the Lamb of God!

If we come to Christ by faith, we shall not die in our sins. Like Noah in the ark, we shall be safe, while unbelievers eternally perish.

As Noah therefore prepared the ark, so should you come to the Ark prepared for you; even Christ Jesus. Ask of God to give you that preparation of heart, by which you will be inclined to receive Christ. Pray for faith, and holy fear, and power to love and serve your Saviour: pray for perseverance, and willingness to bear reproach for His name's sake.—And O! if possible, prevail on others to enter into the same Ark with you, that they also may be saved.

PRAYER.

O Lord, who hast provided for us in Christ Jesus a way of life and salvation: We beseech thee, suffer us not to live as those who know thee not; but lead us, by thy Holy Spirit, to come out and be separate from this present evil world. Save us from impenitence and hardness of heart: quicken our steps, that we may flee unto Jesus, who delivereth us from the wrath to come; and let us not perish with the multitudes that forget God.

O Lord God Almighty, our Saviour and our Judge: we know neither the day nor the hour when thou wilt come. Keep us ever watchful, and ready for thy coming. May we always stand prepared, with our loins girded about, and our lights burning, as those who wait for their Lord.

Bless us in our endeavours to bring men to the knowledge of salvation. If any scorn our words, enable us still, with all gentleness and long-suffering, to entreat them, for Christ's sake, to be reconciled unto thee.

Hear us, O our Heavenly Father; and so guide and keep us in this world, that in the last Great Day we fail not of everlasting life. All which we ask for Jesus Christ's sake, our only Saviour and Redeemer. Amen.

ABRAHAM OFFERING UP ISAAC.
Genesis xxii. 1—12.

And it came to pass, after these things, that God did tempt Abraham; and said unto him, Abraham: and he said, Behold, here I am.

And he said, Take now thy son, thine only son Isaac, whom thou lovest, and get thee into the land of Moriah; and offer him there for a burnt-offering, upon one of the mountains which I will tell thee of.

And Abraham rose up early in the morning, and saddled his ass, and took two of his young men with him, and Isaac his son; and clave the wood for the burnt-offering, and rose up, and went unto the place of which God had told him.

Then on the third day Abraham lift up his eyes, and saw the place afar off.

GENESIS XXII. 1—12. 43

And Abraham said unto his young men, Abide ye here with the ass; and I and the lad will go yonder and worship, and come again to you.

And Abraham took the wood of the burnt offering, and laid it upon Isaac his son; and he took the fire in his hand, and a knife; and they went both of them together.

And Isaac spake unto Abraham his father, and said, My father: and he said, Here am I, my son. And he said, Behold, the fire and the wood; but where is the lamb for a burnt-offering?

And Abraham said, My son, God will provide himself a lamb for a burnt-offering: so they went both of them together.

And they came to the place which God had told him of: and Abraham built an altar there, and laid the wood in order, and bound Isaac his son, and laid him on the altar upon the wood.

And Abraham stretched forth his hand, and took the knife to slay his son.

And the angel of the LORD called unto him out of heaven, and said, Abraham, Abraham: and he said, Here am I.

And he said, Lay not thine hand upon the lad, neither do thou any thing unto him: for now I know that thou fearest God, seeing thou hast not withheld thy son, thine only son, from me.

IT is said at the beginning of this chapter, that "God did tempt Abraham:" which does not signify that He tempted him to commit sin: "for God cannot be tempted with evil, neither tempteth he any man." But it means, that God *tried* him:—so St. Paul expresses it (Hebrews xi. 17.): "By faith Abraham, when he was tried, offered up Isaac."

The faith and obedience of Abraham were indeed put to the severest trial, by this unexpected command of God. Let us observe the circumstances of this history: and may the Holy Spirit enable us to profit by it!

1. In the first place, Abraham, the father of the

faithful, had his *faith* put to a severe proof by this trial. No doubt he fully understood that the command came immediately from God: " Take now thy son, thine only son Isaac, whom thou lovest, and get thee into the land of Moriah; and offer him there for a burnt-offering, upon one of the mountains which I will tell thee of." That voice, which formerly had promised the birth of Isaac, was well known to Abraham: and it is the same voice that now bids him sacrifice Isaac. He would naturally be led to reason within himself— " How can this be? This beloved child is the son of promise, in whom all the nations of the earth are to be blessed; and yet, I am to sacrifice him!"— The apostle Paul tells us how Abraham overcame this doubt. It was " by faith;"—" accounting that God was able to raise him up, even from the dead." And his faith was so strong, that, when they drew near to the appointed mountain, and even when Isaac made the inquiry with touching simplicity, " Behold the fire and the wood; but where is the lamb for a burnt-offering?" Abraham mildly replied, " My son, God will provide himself a lamb for a burnt-offering."

2. The *obedience* of Abraham was also tried by this command. Although fully convinced in his mind that the command came from God, yet he might have felt unwilling to obey. He might have said thus within himself:—" This is God's command; but it is too severe, too hard to be obeyed!" Instead of believing that God still intended mercy,

he might have felt—" I serve a hard master, who will be content with nothing less than my dearest child." Or he might have argued within himself— " What will Sarah, my wife, say? and my servants —and my pious friends—and my ungodly acquaintance?—and what will Isaac himself say or do, on this trying occasion?" All this, and much more, might have agitated his mind, both at the first, and during the three days they were on the journey. Yet, he obeys. He finally lays Isaac upon the altar; and binds him, and stretches forth his hand, and takes the knife to slay his son.

God having thus proved Abraham's faith and obedience, and found his servant " not wanting," restrains him, by an angel's voice, from killing Isaac; accepts another offering; and renews his covenant of blessing, with the most solemn words of approbation and favour:—" By myself have I sworn, saith the LORD, for because thou hast done this thing, and hast not withheld thy son, thine only son; that in blessing I will bless thee, and in multiplying I will multiply thy seed as the stars of the heaven, and as the sand which is upon the seashore; and thy seed shall possess the gate of his enemies: and in thy seed shall all the nations of the earth be blessed; because thou hast obeyed my voice."

What lessons, then, are *we* to learn from this history?

Though not called in the same manner with Abraham to offer a sacrifice, we may be called to suffer a loss; one possibly as severe as his. We may have to part with a child, or a most beloved relative, or some object most tenderly valued by us. What, in such a case, does Abraham's example teach us?

1. It teaches us, that in our bitterest griefs we should exercise unshaken faith in the wisdom, love, and goodness of our Heavenly Father. Did Abraham readily offer up his only son, the son of promise?—and shall not we submit to the appointment of our God, who hath promised to make "all things work together for good to them that love Him?" If we cannot see the hand of a gracious Father in our heaviest trials, where is our faith?

2. Further—The example of Abraham reminds us of other graces which we have to exercise, when tried by afflictions, bereavements, and losses. Humble resignation is the grace which we are then called to exercise. Outwardly we may seem to have no very active duty, no very severe task to perform—no three-days' journey—no binding of Isaac to the altar—no stretching forth of our hand to take the sacrificing knife. But, we have to resist the inward struggles of the soul—meekly to take up our cross day after day—to bind down our stubborn will—to subdue the discontented affections—to mortify our murmuring thoughts! This is hard work! but it is dutiful obedience: it is humble resignation. Thus afflictions discover how far we can obey and submit to our Father's holy will. Can we kiss the chastening rod? Can we part with

the beloved idol? Can we give up to God our Isaac, concerning whom we had made to ourselves so many fond and endearing promises? Can we silence our most heart-rending sorrows with—"It is the Lord: let Him do what seemeth him good"? Oh, that we had more of Abraham's spirit—the spirit of faith, obedience, and resignation!

But let us compare with this touching history, one which is far more affecting and important—the history of the voluntary sacrifice of the Son of God for the redemption of mankind. Did Abraham cheerfully proceed to offer up his only-begotten son Isaac? Let this remind us of the amazing love of God the Father. " He spared not his own Son, but delivered him up for us all." Did Isaac meekly surrender himself? Let this remind us of our Redeemer's willingness to be made a sacrifice for man's sin. His language, on coming into the world for our salvation, was— " Lo, I come to do thy will, O my God." And again he says, " Therefore doth my Father love me, because I lay down my life, that I might take it again. No man taketh it from me, but I lay it down of myself. I have power to lay it down, and I have power to take it again." This story of Abraham and Isaac is indeed a bright emblem of the history of man's redemption by Christ Jesus. To Jesus, therefore, be all glory and praise. He is our atoning Priest, our willing sacrifice, our spotless burnt-offering, who was wholly consumed for us.

He suffered the bitter death of the cross for our salvation. He is now ascended on high, and is able to save to the uttermost all that come unto God by him. To Jesus, the Son of God, be glory in the Church, throughout all ages, world without end. Amen.

PRAYER.

O Lord our Heavenly Father, who sparedst not thine own Son, but didst freely give him up for us all: how shalt thou not with Him also freely give us all things? We beseech thee to endue us with a constant and lively faith in him. Since He died and rose again, and is set down at the right hand of thy throne, may we ever look up to Him as our Intercessor and Advocate with thee, and obtain the petitions which we offer unto thee, in his name.

We know not what thou mayest call us to surrender to thee. But we acknowledge Thee as the rightful owner of all that we have, and are. O fill us with thy Spirit, making us obedient to thy commands, and resigned to thy wise and holy dispensations. May we love and desire nothing so much, as that thy will may be done, and thy name glorified, in us and by us. And finally, O Lord, after that we have suffered awhile, make us to be partakers of thine eternal rest, and to sit down with Abraham, Isaac and Jacob, and with all the saints of God, in thy kingdom in heaven; there to join in adoring the Father, the Son, and the Holy Ghost, for ever and ever. Amen.

XI.

JACOB'S LADDER.
Genesis xxviii. 10—22.

And Jacob went out from Beersheba, and went toward Haran.

And he lighted upon a certain place, and tarried there all night, because the sun was set: and he took of the stones of that place, and put them for his pillows, and lay down in that place to sleep.

And he dreamed, and behold, a ladder set up on the earth, and the top of it reached to heaven; and, behold, the angels of God ascending and descending on it.

And, behold, the Lord stood above it, and said, I am the Lord God of Abraham thy father, and the God of Isaac: the land whereon thou liest, to thee will I give it, and to thy seed:

And thy seed shall be as the dust of the earth; and thou shalt spread abroad to the west, and to the east, and to the north, and to the south: and in thee and in thy seed shall all the families of the earth be blessed.

And, behold, I am with thee, and will keep thee in all places whither thou goest, and will bring thee again into this land: for I will not leave thee, until I have done that which I have spoken to thee of.

And Jacob awaked out of his sleep; and he said, Surely the Lord is in this place; and I knew it not.

And he was afraid, and said, How dreadful is this place! this is none other but the house of God, and this is the gate of heaven.

And Jacob rose up early in the morning, and took the stone that he had put for his pillows, and set it up for a pillar, and poured oil upon the top of it.

And he called the name of that place, Beth-el: but the name of that city was called Luz at the first.

And Jacob vowed a vow, saying, If God will be with me, and will keep me in this way that I go, and will give me bread to eat, and raiment to put on,

So that I come again to my father's house in peace; then shall the Lord be my God.

And this stone, which I have set for a pillar, shall be God's house: and of all that thou shalt give me, I will surely give the tenth unto thee.

WE can scarcely conceive a more sad condition for a good man to be in, than that in which Jacob was placed. He was on a sudden under the necessity of quitting his home: he was lonely, with a long journey before him: his mind saddened by the remembrance of his own and his mother's deceit; and haunted by the fear of his brother, who threatened some day to murder him. At length, wearied by the first day's travel, he lays himself down, with a stone for his pillow, and falls asleep.

He had, indeed, one comfort; and the consolation was truly a holy one—the blessing of his good father, Isaac: a blessing given before, and now more solemnly confirmed to him upon his departure. This furnished him with matter for prayer and praise: and probably his evening's devotions, before he lay down, were greatly assisted by meditatation on this fatherly blessing.

Our waking thoughts often find their way into our dreams: but Jacob's was a special case: it pleased God, by a miraculous vision, to raise his heart to the highest pitch of assurance and peace. As he slept, behold a Ladder, reaching from earth to heaven. This signified the unceasing care of God for his people. The angels, ascending and descending upon the ladder, were the Ministers of God's Providence, ministers of mercy.

By the help of a passage in St. John's Gospel,

we learn, that it is through the Mediator, Christ Jesus, that the care of the Lord is vouchsafed to his children on earth. For Jesus expressly says to Nathanael, in words plainly referring to Jacob's vision—" Hereafter ye shall see heaven open, and the angels of God ascending and descending upon the Son of Man."

The Lord Jesus himself, therefore, was here presented to Jacob's faith, under the similitude of a Ladder. For through our Redeemer it is, that we, fallen and wretched sinners, may obtain reconciliation with God. Through Christ we may draw near to our Father on high. We may, as it were, climb up from earth to heaven, from a state of ruin to salvation, from sin to holiness. Not only are we permitted—we are encouraged, yea, commanded— thus to believe in Christ. And they who, in this appointed way, draw nigh unto God, are kept by him with the most tender, fatherly care. They may sometimes be miserably lodged, scantily fed, sorely persecuted, or deeply afflicted: yea, their sins may often be visited with deserved chastisements, as Jacob's were: still, they are bound to trust in Jesus, and not be afraid. If they commit their ways unto the Lord, their thoughts shall be established. In the lonely and dark night they shall find the Lord to be very nigh unto them, full of grace and pity.

Jacob had special promises that the land of Canaan should be his—that his family should be numerous (though as yet he was an unmarried man)

—that the Redeemer should spring from him—and that the Lord would be with him in all places whither he should go. We, like Jacob, have also the promise of all real good, in and through Christ: the heavenly Canaan shall be ours: the presence of the Lord, by his Spirit, shall accompany us. " He hath said, I will never leave thee nor forsake thee: so that we may boldly say, The Lord is my helper, and I will not fear what man shall do unto me."

Perhaps you are poor, or desolate, or disconsolate, or in many ways deeply afflicted. Look upward, through Jesus, and behold on high the God of Jacob. Trust Him as *your* God. He will send his angels to compass you round about, to defend you, and to minister unto you. Were you even so destitute, so unbefriended, and so sickly, as actually to die of disease and want; still, if you be a true believer in Jesus, angels would immediately be in readiness, to carry you, like Lazarus, into Abraham's bosom.

O think, when you are downcast—" Assuredly I have on high such a Friend, such a Father, as Jacob had;—a Saviour, who loves and pities me, and who will not suffer my soul to perish! This is comfort enough, in the midst of all my sufferings and sorrows!"

It is an awful, yet it is a blessed thing, to feel that God is near. So Jacob felt it. He calls his lonely resting-place, " the house of God," " the gate of heaven." The poorest chamber, a solitary spot in the fields, a bed of sickness or of death, has been to many a believer, " the gate of heaven!" For wherever Christ is revealed to the eye of faith, there heavenly joy opens on the soul.

Have *you* known Christ in this manner? Have you felt him to be precious, as the Mediator through whom your prayers are heard and answered? Then, like Jacob, rise and worship Him anew; and vow, and pay unto Him your vows. How moderate, how humble, how simple and devout were Jacob's petitions! Four things he asks—The Presence of God in his journey out: Food; Raiment; and a Return in safety home. How large his vow—To serve the Lord—to worship him again in that very place—and to honour him with the tenth part of all his substance. It is right, when we are afflicted, that we should in a more especial manner pray and vow unto the Lord. But, oh! how needful is it, that, when God has been gracious to us, we should remember our vows! Jacob, as the history afterwards relates, was somewhat forgetful and negligent of this duty. Oh may God make, and also keep us faithful, humble, and thankful!

PRAYER.

O Lord, who art nigh unto them that call upon thee, to all that call upon thee in truth: Help us, at all times and in all places, to approach thee with lively faith, through Jesus the Mediator of the new covenant. In him thou hast given unto us far better promises than were enjoyed by thy servants of old. Oh, may we ever look up to Jesus for grace to blot out all our sins, for wisdom to direct our path, and for the gift of the Holy Spirit to enlighten, sanctify, and comfort our souls, while we are journeying through this dark and sinful world.

Deliver us, good Lord, from all those evils which we, through our sins, most righteously have deserved. Give us wisdom to live peaceably with all men: and do thou make all men to be at peace with us. Give thy holy angels charge concerning us, to keep us in every right way wherein we go. Yea, be Thou thyself, O God, ever with us, as thou hast promised to be with them that love and serve and worship Thee. Should poverty or distress be our portion, then let thy comforts refresh our souls. Make us rich in grace: and be Thou to us, more than all the good which this perishing world can bestow.

Lord, teach us to be contented with all thy dispensations: and enable us to glorify thee by a holy use of thy manifold and undeserved benefits. May we choose Thee for our portion while we live: and when we die, may we enter in through the gate of the heavenly city, the Jerusalem which is above; there to dwell and reign, together with thy saints, in glory everlasting, through Christ our Lord. Amen.

JOSEPH AND HIS BRETHREN.

Genesis xlv. 1—8.

Then Joseph could not refrain himself before all them that stood by him; and he cried, Cause every man to go out from me. And there stood no man with him, while Joseph made himself known unto his brethren.

And he wept aloud: and the Egyptians and the house of Pharaoh heard.

And Joseph said unto his brethren, I am Joseph: doth my father yet live? And his brethren could not answer him: for they were troubled at his presence.

And Joseph said unto his brethren, Come near to me, I pray you: and they came near: and he said, I am Joseph your brother, whom ye sold in Egypt.

Now therefore be not grieved, nor angry with yourselves, that ye sold me hither; for God did send me before you, to preserve life.

For these two years hath the famine been in the land: and yet there are five years, in the which there shall neither be earing nor harvest.

And God sent me before you, to preserve you a posterity in the earth, and to save your lives by a great deliverance.

So now it was not you that sent me hither, but God: and he hath made me a father to Pharaoh, and lord of all his house, and a ruler throughout all the land of Egypt.

THE history of Joseph is well known to all readers of the Bible. It is so beautifully simple, that even children are charmed with it: and so instructive, that the oldest and the wisest may profit by it.

In this part of the history we may learn, first, to admire the Providence of God in taking care of Joseph. Next, observe the merciful disposition of this good man; in which he was a type of our

Lord Jesus Christ. May the Lord himself be our Teacher, that we may feel the lessons thus set before us!

1. Observe, in the case of Joseph, the wonderful Providence of God. Throughout the whole of his course, those words of David are shown to be true: " The steps of a good man are ordered by the Lord." Let us notice a few of his steps.

What a mournful and disastrous morning was that on which Joseph left his father's house, to go and seek his brethren! His father had been overfond of him, and therefore his brethren hated him; and, as soon as they saw him coming near, plotted his death. A solemn warning this to parents, not to show a liking for any of their children above the others: it only creates heart-burnings.

In what distress must Joseph have been, when his brethren spoke of killing him: they saw the anguish of his soul, when he besought them, but they would not hear. Presently, in part through a secret relenting, and partly through selfishness, they were persuaded to spare his life, and sell him to the Ishmaelites.

And now that he is carried down into Egypt, and sold to a new master, and then shamefully slandered and cast into prison, every thing, for thirteen long and miserable years, seems to be against him. At length the time came that his cause was known; and he was brought out of prison, and in a short time made governor of all the land of Egypt.

Now began the favourable turn in his affairs.

He had been delivered from a violent death, from temptation to sin, and from unrighteous imprisonment: and he is at length made a blessing to immense multitudes, who otherwise must have perished by famine.

All this he ascribes to God. Walking "by faith," at every step he had been led by an unseen hand. This faith he avowed: for when Pharaoh sent for him to interpret his dream, Joseph meekly and devoutly answered, "It is not in me: God shall send Pharaoh an answer of peace." And here before his brethren he declares, "So now it was not you that sent me hither, but God."

Oh, let us learn to say, when cast into a long course of trials—not, "All these things are against me"—but, "We know that all things work together for good to them that love God, to them that are the called according to his purpose." And when we review difficulties, and see how we have been delivered, let us acknowledge, "Not my power, not my skill—but thine arm, O Lord, and thy wisdom, brought about my deliverance, because Thou hadst a favour unto me."

Every man on earth—all families, and all nations—should look up to God as their only sufficient protector, and their all-wise guide. "The Lord preserveth all them that love Him:"—words very simple, but most encouraging to all believers!

2. In the merciful disposition of Joseph towards his brethren, let us observe how greatly he resembles our divine Redeemer, Christ Jesus.

Joseph now had it in his power to take revenge upon his guilty brethren. He might starve them, or imprison them, or order them away for execution. Benjamin alone excepted, they richly deserved punishment; for they had been, all but actual murderers. Instead of this, however, his bowels yearn over them: he weeps for joy at the sight of them: he calls them near to him: he entreats them to fear nothing: he forgives them: he kisses them; and again weeps over them. He bids them look higher than their own sins, higher than his own princely dignity, as high as the mercy-seat itself, to the great God of all, their Judge and their Redeemer.

What, my friend, do we see in this, but a picture of what Jesus does on our behalf? This is the very way in which He welcomes penitent, returning sinners, though by their sins they crucified him. Thus it is that He forgives, blots out, aad remembers no more, our transgressions. Thus it is that He bids us come near to him, that he may comfort us, put on us the robe of his righteousness, and treat us as beloved brethren. He rejoices over us, to do us good. Like Joseph's brethren, indeed, we ought never to forget our own unworthiness: but, being encouraged even more than they were, we ought never to distrust the assurances of Jesus. We should cast ourselves freely into the arms of his mercy, and accept, without the least doubting, the abundance of His grace.

Thus let us learn to sing both of the providence

of our God, and also of the loving-kindness of Jesus.
The following hymn suits both subjects.

> This God is the God we adore,
>   Our faithful, unchangeable Friend;
> Whose love is as great as his power,
>   And knows neither measure nor end.
>
> 'Tis Jesus, the first and the last,
>   Whose Spirit shall guide us safe home:
> We'll praise Him for all that is past,
>   And trust Him for all that's to come.

PRAYER.

O Lord, who never failest to help and govern them whom thou dost bring up in thy steadfast fear and love: Keep us, we beseech thee, under the protection of thy good Providence, and make us to have a perpetual fear and love of thy holy name. Fill us with the grace of thy Holy Spirit, that we may be kept from sinning against thee. Cause us to remember that thine eye is in every place, beholding the evil and the good. Comfort us by the assurance that thine ears are open unto the prayers of those who ask in Thy Son's name; and that thou wilt withhold no good thing from them that walk uprightly.

O Lord of Hosts, blessed is the man that trusteth in thee. Enable us, with unshaken faith, to cast all our cares upon Thee, who carest for us. Among all the changes of this mortal life, O keep our souls in quietness and patience, looking for thy loving-kindness and faithfulness, which thou wilt in due time manifest to all that wait on thee.

Remember, O Lord, the word unto thy servants, in which thou hast caused us to hope; and answer us according to the multitude of thy mercies, through Jesus Christ, our Saviour and Redeemer. Amen.

XIII.
A FATHER'S BLESSING.
Genesis xlviii. 14—16.

And Israel stretched out his right hand, and laid it upon Ephraim's head, who was the younger; and his left hand upon Manasseh's head; guiding his hands wittingly; for Manasseh was the first-born.

And he blessed Joseph, and said, God, before whom my fathers Abraham and Isaac did walk, the God which fed me all my life long unto this day,

The Angel which redeemed me from all evil, bless the lads; and let my name be named on them, and the name of my fathers Abraham and Isaac; and let them grow into a multitude in the midst of the earth.

WHEN pious parents feel the day of their death drawing nigh, they should ponder well how they may do the most good to their children, and children's children. A few words spoken at such a time sink deep into the hearts of the young: they touch bystanders also, who enjoy the privilege of hearing the last counsel of dying saints. Thus did Jacob bless his twelve sons, just before he died: and some little time earlier than that, he had his two grandchildren brought to him by their father, the tenderly-beloved Joseph; and he blessed them in the words just now read to you.

Let us meditate on the thoughts suggested by this fatherly blessing.

1. First, we see how Jacob *remembers the Covenant* made by the Lord with his fathers. The Covenant made with Abraham was, that in his Seed all the nations of the earth should be blessed. This Seed was Jesus Christ. He sprang from Abraham; and He alone is the source of all blessing: He is the Angel of the everlasting Covenant of Peace between God and man. This Covenant had been embraced and faithfully kept by Abraham and Isaac; and here Jacob solemnly records the fact: "God, before whom my fathers Abraham and Isaac did walk."

What a blessing is it, my friend, to be descended from pious parents aad ancestors! Yet, even if we have not been so remarkably favoured as Jacob, who had a pious Abraham for his grandfather, and a pious Isaac for his father; still we may lay claim to the everlasting Covenant, ordered in all things and sure, sealed with the blood of our crucified Redeemer. Oh let us, when we come to die, remember Jesus Christ, who purchased our redemption with His blood! Let us exalt Him: let us invite our families and our friends to trust in his Cross: let our lips continually speak of His love; and let our last breath be a Hallelujah to the name of Jesus!

2. Next, observe how Jacob *records the mercies* of his past life. Often had he been reduced to the greatest distress, through oppression, famine, and

dangers of various kinds. His days had been "few and evil." Yet the Lord had fed him all his life long, and had redeemed him from all evil. We, in like manner, ought to call to mind our many past mercies, that we may encourage those who come after, to trust in the Lord; even in Him who hath promised, "I will never leave thee, nor forsake thee."—Jacob refers also to our Lord Jesus Christ, when he says, "The Angel which redeemed me from all evil." What a comfort, to be able to think and speak of a Redeemer, in a dying hour! To whom shall we commend our children and our dearest friends, but to Jesus, the All-sufficient, the never-failing Helper, Rock, and Refuge of our souls?

3. Then comes *the solemn benediction:*—Oh may this Angel of the Covenant, the faithful Redeemer of my soul, "BLESS THE LADS." Words, few and simple; yet most tender, weighty, and expressive! It was not a mere common way of speaking, when the venerable saint said, "Bless the lads!" Many say, "God bless you," almost without a thought. Not so Jacob. Methinks, as the old man pronounced those words over his two granchildren, the grace of God must have touched their souls like a magnet, drawing them heavenward.—Jacob seems to say to them, "Look up, beloved youth's; yes, look upward to our Great Redeemer, the Author and Finisher of our faith! He has been *my* Comforter; may He be *yours*! His blessing abide with both of you now and for ever!"

He declares, also, that his own name, and the names of his fathers, Abraham and Isaac, shall be named on these, his two grandchildren: and he prophesies that they shall grow into a multitude in the midst of the earth. Thus would the promises made to Abraham be fulfilled, that his seed should be "as the stars of heaven for multitude."

Such is the manner in which the dying Patriarch blesses his son's children. Let us learn from his example, how to bid a last farewell, profitably, to those whom we love.—O my friend, life is short, and death is drawing nearer every hour. Let us look round on the circle of our relatives, and let our love for them be sanctified by the spirit of prayer! Let us entreat God to bestow on every one of them His saving grace! Then, as we depart this life, we may say to them—" I have often prayed for you, dear friends, while I was in health: and now, that I feel myself to be dying, my chief comfort on your behalf, is, still to pray for you. Oh let me, with my latest breath, commend you to God, and to the word of His grace; which is able to build you up, and to give you an inheritance among all them that are sanctified!"

PRAYER.

Lord, thou hast been our dwelling-place in all generations. Thy saints have put their trust under the shadow of thy wings, and have found rest and safety in thee. Thou hast taught them from their youth, and even to hoar hairs thou hast carried them. Thou pardonest all our iniquities through the atoning blood of Jesus. Thou renewest thine image in the soul of every believer: and thou freely givest thy Holy Spirit to them that ask thee.

Be thou, Lord, a protector, a guide and comforter to us, as thou hast been to thy servants of old. Feed us with food convenient for us: be with us in the way wherein we go: deliver us from all evil: shine upon us with the light of thy countenance; and give unto us the joys of thy salvation.

Cause the blessings of the everlasting Covenant to descend, O Lord, and rest upon children, and children's children, even throughout all generations. Pour thy Spirit upon the offspring of thy faithful servants; that they may spring up as fruitful trees, the planting of the Lord, that thou mayest be glorified. Incline their hearts to love and serve thee. Let one say, I am the Lord's; and another call himself by the name of Jacob; and another subscribe with his hand unto the Lord, and surname himself by the name of Israel. Bless them, O Lord, and make them a blessing: and grant that there may never be wanting a seed to serve thee on earth. And, finally, gather thy faithful children together in one, to surround thy throne of glory, through Jesus Christ our Lord and our Redeemer. Amen.

XIV.
THE LAST FAREWELL.
Genesis xlix. 33.

And when Jacob had made an end of commanding his sons, he gathered up his feet into the bed, and yielded up the ghost, and was gathered unto his people.

THE life of Jacob was marked by many changes. His dwelling-place on earth was very unsettled, and he seems like a man that, at one spot or another, was perpetually bidding Farewell. His heart, however, was fixed;—it was securely fixed on his Covenant God and Saviour. As he draws nearer to his end, he manifests the greatest assurance of faith. We here see him, on his death-bed, with his twelve sons gathered round him to receive his blessing; while he, holy man, pauses a moment in the middle of his address to them, that he may utter those memorable words—" I have waited for thy salvation, O Lord."

Let us go briefly through his history, regarding it as a continual series of separations: noticing how frequently he had to take leave, first of one place or person, then of another; closing with his last Farewell.

1. First, he quitted home (Genesis xxvii. 41—45), being sent away, because his mother feared lest Esau, his brother, should perform a threat of murdering Jacob. This was a season of deep disgrace, alarm, and grief. He had deceived his father, and supplanted his brother: and now he parts

from home under conscious guilt. His mother bids him—" Flee to Haran, and tarry there a few days." Alas! it proved an absence of more than twenty years; and we do not read that he ever saw his mother again.

2. The second parting was, when he fled from Laban: (Genesis xxxi. 17—24.) In this instance, it was not with Jacob that the fault lay. His father-in-law, Laban, was a selfish, unreasonable man; and had oppressed him and his family. Jacob fled from him, was pursued, and overtaken: but God, in a night-vision, spake to Laban, and restrained him from hurting his son-in-law;—so that the next morning they parted as friends.

3. The next was a politic separation: (Genesis xxxiii. 16, 17.) After an absence of above twenty years, he again saw his brother Esau; who came to meet him with four hundred armed men; so that Jacob had good cause to fear, lest now, at length, his brother should cut him off. But, in answer to Jacob's prayer, the Lord softened the cruel heart of Esau. They met as friends; but only for one day: for on the day following, Jacob quietly departed; being fearful, perhaps, lest his brother's friendship should not last very long. For it is most true, " A brother offended is harder to be won than a city that hath bars and bolts." And when he is won, still great caution is necessary afterwards, lest new offences should arise.

4. Jacob's next remarkable move was from Shechem, in terror and family-disgrace; his daughter

Dinah having been shamefully treated, and his two sons, Simeon and Levi, having wreaked their vengeance by murdering all the men of that city. And now it is that Jacob is reminded of his promises to God, made well nigh thirty years before; and goes to Bethel, to perform his solemn vow: (Genesis xxxv. 1.)

5. Soon after, there was a parting with an aged nurse, Deborah: (Genesis xxxv. 8.) As the Holy Spirit has caused this simple event to be recorded, it is probable that there was something peculiarly excellent in the character of this good old domestic. Aged servants, who have kept their proper place in the family, and have served well, are indeed truly valuable, and worthy of much honour. Deborah was buried under an oak; and they lamented for her, and called the name of the place Allon-bachuth: that is, 'The oak of weeping.'

6. A very bitter parting was the next, when Jacob was bereft of his beloved wife, Rachel: (Genesis xxxv. 16—20.) It was a farewell, too, at a very short warning; for she died in child-birth. This stroke cut deep indeed! Perhaps the wound was never quite healed: for not long before his own death, as he was speaking to his son Joseph on family-matters, Jacob could not help sighing out —"As for me, when I came from Padan, Rachel died by me in the land of Canaan in the way, when yet there was but a little way to come unto Ephrath: and I buried her there, in the way of Ephrath; the same is Bethlehem."

7. After this, there was a parting with his aged father, Isaac: (Genesis xxxv. 27—29.) "His sons, Esau and Jacob, buried him." The last time that these two sons had together been with their father, was probably more than forty years before; on the day when Jacob had deceived his father, and had thereby supplanted and enraged his brother Esau. It is true, Esau had been reconciled to him more than half that space of time. But, oh! what bitter, what humbling recollections must have rushed into Jacob's mind, while attending, with Esau, the funeral of their father!

8. And now comes a heavy blow on Jacob's fond and fatherly heart. He sends his favourite son, Joseph, into the country, to seek for his brethren. They seize him; sell him; and then bring back a false story to their father, which leaves his mind under the full impression that Joseph had been devoured by a wild beast! Cruel brothers! deceitful sons! And yet deceit had been the early crime of Jacob too. As he had sinned to his father, in like manner do his sons, by lying, now sin against him. Jacob refuses to be comforted. He cries, "I will go down into the grave unto my son, mourning." "Thus his father wept for him."— This was indeed a sudden and a tremendous separation! (Genesis xxxvii. 35.)

9. After many years, Jacob is forced to part with nearly all his family. This famine was sore in the land of Canaan, where he dwelt; and he must needs send all his sons, save one, to go down into

Egypt to buy corn: as he piteously says, "That we may live, and not die:" (Genesis xlii. 2.)

10. Next came, sore against his will, the necessity for parting with Benjamin. He argued, and struggled hard against this necessity; but could not help himself: (Genesis xlviii. 11—14.) At last he yields: but adds this tender, fatherly prayer:— " And God Almighty give you mercy before the man, that he may send away your other brother, and Benjamin. If I be bereaved of my children, I am bereaved!"—His lamentation showed weakness of spirits: but his petition is a model for *us*, should we be constrained at any time to part with our children under trying circumstances.

11. In the next instance, we find Jacob breaking up his whole family-establishment at once; leaving Canaan, the land of promise; and going down into Egypt with all his household. Affairs had taken a most surprising turn. Joseph, his son, is yet alive: and Jacob is invited to come and spend the remainder of his days with this beloved son, now governor of all the land of Egypt. Having performed a solemn "sacrifice unto the God of his father Isaac," he departs with a glad heart to Joseph in Egypt: (Genesis xlvi. 1—7.)

12. At length, his life drawing to a close, he bids a more private, personal adieu to Joseph and his two sons: (Genesis xlvii. 27—31. and xlviii.) On this occasion he charges his son to carry his bones to the cave of Machpelah, the burying-place of Abraham and Isaac. His very bones refuse

to rest in heathenish Egypt, and seek repose in Canaan. This was a token of his confidence that his seed should, in God's good time, possess the promised inheritance. On the same occasion, he blesses his grandchildren, Ephraim and Manasseh, in words which cannot be read without tears; at least by those who have shared in any measure the experience of Jacob. "God, before whom my fathers, Abraham and Isaac, did walk; the God which fed me all my life long unto this day; the Angel which relieved me from all evil, BLESS THE LADS!"

13. Yet further, there is his dying Farewell to his twelve sons, assembled round his bed. In these his last words we find weighty reproof united with tender affection. He mingles great prophecies with earnest prayers and blessings. To the very last he reminds them of their covenanted interest in Canaan: (Genesis xlix.)

14. Finally, observe his Farewell to life itself. Ere he gives up the ghost, he proclaims that he has hope in his death. "I have waited for thy salvation, O Lord." Like his grandfather Abraham, he beholds from afar off the day of Christ: "He saw it, and was glad." Now nothing remains for him, but to gather up his feet into the bed, while his spirit departs to dwell for ever with the Lord. Thus the Patriarch takes his last earthly leave:— "Farewell, my sons, and all my children's children! Farewell, vain, disappointing world! Farewell, thou Church of God on earth! Farewell,

but not for ever! Let us meet again as glorified saints in the everlasting Canaan above; where there shall be no more sin; no more deceit or violence; no more want or famine; no more anguish of heart or pain of body; no more parting tears; no pillar at Rachel's tomb; no grave at Machpelah! There we shall all form one blessed, inseparable family; dwelling in light and love and joy, in the presence of our Redeemer, for ever !"

PRAYER.

Almighty and Ever-living God, who dost make all things work together for good to them that love thee: Enable us, by the power of the Holy Spirit, to die to the world, and live to thy honour and glory. We confess that we are strangers and pilgrims on the earth: oh, may we desire a better country, even an heavenly ! Endue us with a spirit of strong and lively faith, that we may discern between things temporal and things eternal, and never be moved away from the hope of the Gospel. Whatever changes or afflictions may befal us, may they help us in pressing forward to our future inheritance in heaven. Cause us to set our affection constantly on things above, not on things on the earth.

Pardon, good Lord, the many and grievous sins which we have committed against thee, by thought, word, and deed. In every affair of life wherein we have been engaged, and in every place where we have dwelt or visited, some spot of guilt has been upon us; and our very services to thee have been stained with much evil. Our corruptions have many times prevailed against us: our infirmities have bowed us down: our iniquities throughout our whole pilgrimage testify against us. Lord, we humble ourselves before thee. But we bless thy name, that we have a merciful High Priest, even our Lord Jesus Christ, who is the same yesterday, to-day, and for ever; and we plead his precious blood, which was shed for the remission of sin. Blot out our transgressions for His sake; and our iniquities do thou remember no more.

Prepare us, Lord, for a dying hour. Dispose us meekly to resign into thy hands whatever we have in this world. When heart and flesh faileth, be thou the strength of our heart, and our portion for ever. And may we, in departing this life, partake abundantly of that everlasting consolation, and that good hope through grace, which thou hast prepared for all them that wait on thee. We ask it, through Jesus Christ, our Strength and our Redeemer. Amen.

XV.
THE PASSOVER.

Exodus xii. 3—14. and 21—30.

Speak ye unto all the congregation of Israel, saying, In the tenth day of this month they shall take to them every man a lamb, according to the house of their fathers, a lamb for an house:

And if the household be too little for the lamb, let him and his neighbour next unto his house take it, according to the number of the souls; every man according to his eating shall make your count for the lamb.

EXODUS XII. 3—14. & 21—30.

Your lamb shall be without blemish, a male of the first year: ye shall take it out from the sheep, or from the goats:

And ye shall keep it up until the fourteenth day of the same month: and the whole assembly of the congregation of Israel shall kill it in the evening.

And they shall take of the blood, and strike it on the two side posts, and on the upper door-post of the houses wherein they shall eat it.

And they shall eat the flesh in that night, roast with fire, and unleavened bread; and with bitter herbs they shall eat it.

Eat not of it raw, nor sodden at all with water, but roast with fire; his head with his legs, and with the purtenance thereof.

And ye shall let nothing of it remain until the morning; and that which remaineth of it until the morning ye shall burn with fire.

And thus shall ye eat it; with your loins girded, your shoes on your feet, and your staff in your hand; and ye shall eat it in haste: it is the LORD's passover.

For I will pass through the land of Egypt this night, and will smite all the firstborn in the land of Egypt, both man and beast; and against all the gods of Egypt I will execute judgment: I am the LORD.

And the blood shall be to you for a token upon the houses where ye are: and when I see the blood, I will pass over you, and the plague shall not be upon you to destroy you, when I smite the land of Egypt.

And this day shall be unto you for a memorial; and ye shall keep it a feast to the Lord throughout your generations: ye shall keep it a feast by an ordinance for ever.

*　　*　　*　　*　　*

Then Moses called for all the elders of Israel, and said unto them, Draw out and take you a lamb according to your families, and kill the passover.

And ye shall take a bunch of hyssop, and dip it in the blood that is in the bason, and strike the lintel and the two side-posts with the blood that is in the bason: and none of you shall go out at the door of his house until the morning,

For the Lord will pass through to smite the Egyptians; and

when he seeth the blood upon the lintel, and on the two sideposts, the Lord will pass over the door, and will not suffer the destroyer to come in unto your houses to smite you.

And ye shall observe this thing for an ordinance to thee and to thy sons for ever.

And it shall come to pass, when ye be come to the land which the Lord will give you, according as he hath promised, that ye shall keep this service.

And it shall come to pass, when your children shall say unto you, What mean ye by this service?

That ye shall say, It is the sacrifice of the Lord's passover, who passed over the houses of the children of Israel in Egypt, when he smote the Egyptians, and delivered our houses. And the people bowed the head and worshipped.

And the children of Israel went away, and did as the Lord had commanded Moses and Aaron, so did they.

And it came to pass, that at midnight the Lord smote all the firstborn in the land of Egypt, from the firstborn of Pharaoh that sat on his throne unto the firstborn of the captive that was in the dungeon; and all the firstborn of cattle.

And Pharaoh rose up in the night, he and all his servants, and all the Egyptians; and there was a great cry in Egypt: for there was not a house where there was not one dead.

WE have in this part of the Sacred History various important lessons. In the destruction of so many Egyptians, we behold a sure proof that sin will be avenged by an angry God: while the history of the Israelites under Moses, their deliverer, warrants us to expect the salvation of all who believe and obey the word of God. More especially, the appointment of the Passover gives us a lively emblem of the atonement of the Lord Jesus Christ, through which our salvation is obtained. May the grace of Christ our Saviour be with us, while meditating on these subjects!

1. The ungodly, continuing impenitent till death, cannot escape destruction. They die in their sins: consequently, there is no hope for them beyond the grave.

For the most part, however, the ruin of sinners does not come till they have had many warnings. Pharaoh and the Egyptians had already suffered nine plagues, before this dreadful visitation, of the death of all their first-born. Besides suffering not fewer than ten plagues, they had also heard many plain warnings from God, by the voice of Moses and Aaron: moreover, they had experienced repeated deliverances, as often as Moses interceded for them. Still they refused to obey: still Pharaoh replied, "I know not the Lord, neither will I hearken unto his voice."—Even after all this, and when Israel had escaped from Egypt, Pharaoh was determined once more to wage war with God and his people. It ended in his final ruin; he and his army being swallowed up in the depths of the sea. " They sank into the bottom, as a stone." When sinners dare to fight against God, most assuredly God will show himself Master in the end.

Think, O sinner! madly rushing forward in thine iniquities! what wilt thou do in the end thereof? Art thou stronger than God? or do his threatenings of vengeance mean nothing? Art thou determined, after thy hardness and impenitent heart, to treasure up unto thyself wrath against the day of wrath? Despisest thou the riches of his goodness and forbearance and long-suffering? Knowest thou not, that the goodness of God calleth thee to repentance? O beware, lest that sentence come upon thee, "He that, being often reproved, hardeneth his neck, shall suddenly be cut off, and that without remedy!"

2. But, blessed be God! there is a way of salvation for those who are willing to accept it: and of this we have a most lively emblem, in the account of the Passover. Let us observe the various particulars of this account.

—The lamb to be sacrificed in every family, was intended to prefigure Jesus: for He is the Lamb of God, that taketh away the sins of the world.

—This lamb was to be perfect, and without blemish: so was Jesus perfectly holy, harmless, and undefiled, altogether "without sin."

—As the lamb was solemnly to be slain; so also was Jesus to die: and for our sins He did die, even the bitter death of the Cross.

—The lamb was to be eaten with bitter herbs: denoting, that we should be filled with bitter grief for sin, while feeding on Christ in our hearts by a lively faith. Thus, although mourning, we shall be nourished, strengthened and comforted, with all the blessings of his salvation.

— And as the blood of the lamb was to be sprinkled on the door-posts of the houses of the Israelites, in order that the destroying Angel might not smite any one of God's people; so is the atoning blood of Jesus to be sprinkled upon our consciences, that we may obtain remission of our sins, and deliverance from wrath, through him.

—We may further notice the circumstance, that the Israelites were to eat the lamb in haste, with their loins girt, and their shoes on their feet. The reason was, they were to be ready to depart that very night, at a moment's warning. This is intended to represent the eagerness and despatch with which a Christian should shake off the yoke of sin, and break away from the bondage of Satan. He should also stand ready to leave this wicked world; which is to him what the land of Egypt was to Israel. A true Christian desires complete redemption: he longs for the Canaan above: he is in haste to be gone: he only waits for the voice of his Saviour, bidding him "Come." He stands with his loins girt, and his light burning. His affections are already set off, and have reached heaven before him.

Those of the Israelites who believed the word of the Lord by Moses, obeyed. Was there a single soul among them, you ask, who dared to disobey? No, none that we read of. If there were any such, no doubt their families, as well as the Egyptians, were visited that night by the destroying Angel.

But there are many *among us*—awful to think!—who hear the message of reconciliation through Christ Jesus, and yet disbelieve and reject it. Ask your own conscience, my friend, whether you be of that number? Do you still live on, careless, and disobedient to the Saviour of your soul? or have you come to him, mourning for sin, forsaking sin, seeking and finding pardon and peace through faith in Jesus, and striving to live to his glory?

The night of the Passover, as Moses declares, was "a night to be much observed unto the Lord." It was, in fact, kept in remembrance, even to the very time of our Blessed Lord's crucifixion. But the death of Jesus on the Cross is what Christians are bound chiefly to hold in affectionate remembrance. "Christ, our Passover, is sacrificed for us: therefore let us keep the feast."

Nor has our Lord left us without some solemn memorial of his death. The Sacrament of the Lord's Supper is celebrated in the Church, for this very end. If it be asked of us, as of the successive generations of Israel, "What mean ye by this service?" our plain answer is, This sacred rite Jesus himself appointed, on the same night that he was betrayed; saying, "Do this in remembrance of me." "As oft, therefore, as we eat that bread and drink that cup, we do show the Lord's death till He come."

Hasten therefore, my friend, to Jesus, your Redeemer. Believe in him for salvation. By faith receive the sprinkling of his precious blood upon your soul. Present yourself a living sacrifice to him, and serve him in all holy obedience. Quit the ungodly, that you may not perish with them.

And, whenever you come to the Table of the

Lord, to celebrate the great love of Jesus in dying for you, let your heart be broken afresh for sin: then shall your faith be strengthened; your vows and resolutions shall be confirmed; yea, your whole soul shall be inflamed and filled with love to Him, who hath loved us, and hath given himself for us, and hath washed us from our sins in his own blood! Amen.

PRAYER.

O Lord God Almighty, who hast revealed thy wrath against all ungodliness and unrighteousness of men: Give us grace to tremble at thy judgments, and to serve thee acceptably, with reverence and godly fear. O gather not our souls with sinners. Cause us with fear and trembling to come out, and separate ourselves from their company, lest we perish with them eternally.

We thank thee for having made known to us the way of salvation, through thy Son Jesus Christ. Teach and incline our hearts, by thy Holy Spirit, to believe in Jesus our Lord unto life eternal. For he is the very Paschal Lamb which was slain, to take away all sin. Lead us to mourn over those iniquities, for which he died; and to look unto him, and be saved. Sprinkle on our consciences his most precious blood; that, being justified by faith, we may have peace with thee, through Him.

Lord, establish thy servants with grace. Accept our petitions, when we call upon thee in the name of Christ. Shed abroad in our hearts the love of our adorable Saviour. May we go forth to his service, armed with his strength. Enable us, in the power of the Spirit, to tread down all our enemies. Give us victory over the world, the flesh, and the devil: and being kept faithful unto death, may we be received into thy heavenly kingdom, for the sake of the same thy son, Jesus Christ our Lord. Amen.

XVI.

THE PILLAR OF A CLOUD AND OF FIRE.

Exodus xiii. 21, 22.

And the Lord went before them by day in a pillar of a cloud, to lead them the way; and by night in a pillar of fire, to give them light; to go by day and night:

He took not away the pillar of the cloud by day, nor the pillar of fire by night, from before the people.

Among the many miracles wrought by God on behalf of the Israelites, not one was more remarkable than this manifestation of his presence, in the pillar of a cloud and of fire.

Nor only at the beginning of their journey were they thus guided and protected: all through their sojourn in the wilderness, for the space of forty years, they enjoyed this great privilege. Let us consider the several uses of this miracle.

1. First, it was a Token of the Lord's Covenant with Israel.—The promises of that Covenant had been made to Abraham more than four hundred years before. They had never been forgotten by God, during all the sufferings of the Israelites in

Egypt; for when the time of their deliverance had arrived, it is said, that " God heard their groaning, and God remembered his Covenant with Abraham, with Isaac, and with Jacob." As soon, therefore, as the Israelites were brought out of Egypt, they were signally acknowledged as his peculiar people. Thus St. Paul describes their situation: " All our fathers were under the cloud, and all passed through the sea: and were all baptized unto Moses in the cloud and in the sea:" (1 Cor. x. 1, 2.) They were all solemnly reminded of the Covenant, by this miraculous token of God's presence with his servant Moses, and with them.

2. *The Pillar was also a Guide to them.*—Very remarkable is the fact, as stated in the last chapter of Exodus: " When the cloud was taken up from over the tabernacle, the children of Israel went onward in all their journeys: but if the cloud were not taken up, then they journeyed not, till the day that it was taken up." Thus, whether the cloud tarried a few days, or many days, or a month, or a year, it was their constant guide. When it rested, they rested: when it moved, they moved.

3. *It was also their Security.*—This was remarkably the case during their passage through the Red Sea. On that occasion, when Pharaoh and his army were closely pursuing them, it is related, that " the pillar of the cloud went from before their face, and stood behind them. And it came between the camp of the Egyptians, and the camp of Israel: and it

was a cloud of darkness to them, but gave light by night to these: so that the one came not near the other all the night:" (Exodus xiv. 19, 20.) Their safety may be inferred from the prayer of Moses: for whenever the moving of the cloud gave them the order for marching, Moses pronounced these solemn words: " Rise up, Lord, and let thine enemies be scattered; and let them that hate thee, flee before thee. And when it rested, he said, Return, O Lord, unto the many thousands of Israel:" (Num. x. 35, 36.) Thus would they be protected, in answer to prayer.

4. This continued miracle was also well suited to give them Comfort.—As they passed over burning sands by day, the cloud would shelter them from the sun's overpowering heat: while, in the night, the pillar of fire would cheer them with its mild and pleasant glow. The feeling of God's presence, also, is always a comfort to his people.

5. The occasional withdrawing of this miracle would also convey a Rebuke to the Israelites; " for with many of them God was not well pleased." Thus, after the people had sinned in worshipping the golden calf, Moses took the tabernacle, and pitched it without the camp, " afar off from the camp." When he entered the tabernacle, " the cloudy pillar descended, and stood at the door of the tabernacle, and the Lord talked with Moses:" (Exodus xxxiii. 9.) The pillar must have quitted the camp, thus to descend upon the tabernacle at a distance. The people, perceiving that the Lord

was with Moses, and that He had departed from them, " rose up, and worshipped, every man in his tent-door." They acknowledged the rebuke, and humbled themselves.—On another occasion, when a party of the Israelites determined to go forth to battle contrary to the Lord's command, Moses protested to them, saying, " It shall not prosper. Go not up; for the Lord is not among you." There was no prayer to bless them: nor can we suppose that they were guided by the pillar of a cloud. So they were smitten before their enemies. (See also Miriam's case, Numbers xii. 10.)

" Have we"—you will now be ready to ask— " any guidance similar to this, in our journeying through the wilderness of life?" Yes, we have. A miraculous guide, indeed, we have not : but the Lord has given us what is abundantly sufficient for us, in all our ignorance, wants, and helplessness. We have the word of God to teach us; the Spirit of Christ to lead us; the arm of the Almighty to protect us; and the Providence of God, sometimes opening the way, at other times closing it : so that, if we wait upon him in believing prayer, and accept the helps which he offers us, we shall not be suffered greatly to err. If at any time we do miss our way, it proves that we have been negligent in using the means of grace, and have not faithfully hearkened to the voice of the Spirit. If we continue stedfast in God's covenant, he will be true to his promises. Jesus, the Mediator of the New Covenant, will guide, comfort, and defend every one of his people:—and when we decline from him, he will manifest his love by rebuking us. Never will he leave his believing servants: they shall enter the heavenly Canaan; there to dwell in his presence for ever. " For the Lord God is a Sun and a Shield: the Lord will give grace and glory: no good thing will he withhold from them that walk uprightly." " Thou shalt guide me with thy counsel, and afterward receive me to glory."

PRAYER.

O Lord, who hast given unto us thy holy word, to be a light to our feet and a lantern unto our path: Grant to us also the gift of thy Holy Spirit, which thou hast promised to give to them that ask thee. Comfort us with the tokens of thy presence. Lift up upon us the light of thy countenance. Protect us from every evil and from every danger. Let thy voice be heard continually near us, saying, This is the way, walk in it: and suffer us not to turn aside, to the right hand or to the left.

Thou hast declared, O Lord, that as many as thou lovest, thou dost rebuke. Cause us to receive thy chastisements with all humility; and to learn, by them, what is thy will concerning us. And, Lord, increase our faith: that looking up to thee for wisdom to direct our paths, we may go forward with assurance and hope; and may so pass through our earthly pilgrimage, that finally we may attain thy heavenly rest and glory, through Jesus Christ, our Lord and our Redeemer. Amen.

XVII.

THE MANNA.

Exodus xvi. 11—30.

And the Lord spake unto Moses, saying,

I have heard the murmurings of the children of Israel: speak unto them, saying, At even ye shall eat flesh, and in the morning ye shall be filled with bread; and ye shall know that I am the Lord your God.

And it came to pass, that at even the quails came up, and covered the camp: and in the morning the dew lay round about the host.

And when the dew that lay was gone up, behold, upon the face of the wilderness there lay a small round thing, as small as the hoar frost on the ground.

And when the children of Israel saw it, they said one to another, It is Manna: for they wist not what it was. And Moses said unto them, This is the bread which the Lord hath given you to eat.

This is the thing which the Lord hath commanded, Gather of it every man according to his eating, an omer for every man, according to the number of your persons: take ye every man for them which are in his tents.

And the children of Israel did so, and gathered, some more, some less.

And when they did mete it with an omer, he that gathered much had nothing over, and he that gathered little had no lack: they gathered every man according to his eating.

And Moses said, Let no man leave of it till the morning.

Notwithstanding they hearkened not unto Moses; but some of them left of it until the morning, and it bred worms, and stank: and Moses was wroth with them.

And they gathered it every morning, every man according to his eating: and when the sun waxed hot, it melted.

And it came to pass, that on the sixth day they gathered twice as much bread, two omers for one man: and all the rulers of the congregation came and told Moses.

And he said unto them, This is that which the Lord hath said, To-morrow is the rest of the holy sabbath unto the Lord: bake that which ye will bake to-day, and seethe that ye will seethe; and that which remaineth over lay up for you, to be kept until the morning.

And they laid it up till the morning, as Moses bade: and it did not stink, neither was there any worm therein.

And Moses said, Eat that to-day; for to-day is a sabbath unto the Lord: to-day ye shall not find it in the field.

Six days ye shall gather it; but on the seventh day, which is the sabbath, in it there shall be none.

And it came to pass, that there went out some of the peeple on the seventh day for to gather, and they found none.

And the Lord said unto Moses, How long refuse ye to keep my commandments and my laws?

See, for that the Lord hath given you the sabbath, therefore he giveth you on the sixth day the bread of two days: abide ye every man in his place, let no man go out of his place on the seventh day.

So the people rested on the seventh day.

CONSIDERING that multitudes of the Israelites were ungodly, we cannot wonder that they broke out into loud complaints, as soon as they suffered hunger. But as *they* murmured, so are *we* prone to complain, when want and affliction come upon us. Our hearts are not better than theirs: our murmurings are frequently as loud; and, like them, we sometimes cry out, even *against* the Lord.

God was pleased to hearken to the cry of the Israelites on this occasion; and by a miracle he sent them food from heaven:—first, quails; and then the Manna.

Several useful lessons are taught us by this history. Let us pray to God to give us all the instruction and all the comfort designed by it.

1. The first thing taught us, is, a humbling lesson concerning our Unbelief. We naturally distrust God. Though he has fed us all our life long to this day, yet, the moment trials come upon us, we quickly lose sight of his past mercies, and give way to the gloomy fear, that God has forgotten to be gracious.

2. Nor is this the whole of the evil in our hearts. We wish to be independent—or, at least, to feel and fancy ourselves independent—even of God himself. This is the secret cause, why men desire riches, and dread poverty. They would have goods laid up for years to come: they cannot bear to be held down to the petition, "Give us this day our daily bread."

3. Another affecting lesson to be learnt from the history of the Manna, is, that we are too much inclined to long for what are called the good things of the world. We wish to have dainties: and when we have them not, we pine after them. Thus the children of Israel spoke out their mind plainly, when they murmured after the good things of Egypt: "There," say they, "we sat by the flesh-pots, and did eat bread to the full." What they said in words, every carnal heart feels.

These three sins—a spirit of Unbelief, a spirit of Independence, and a spirit of Self-indulgence—are very deeply seated in the human heart. Have *you* never felt them? Do they not spring up, by turns, again and again? Are you not, perhaps, at this very time, yielding to them?

4. But there is another, and a very cheering

lesson, to be learned from this story. It is—that the Lord will not fail to supply the wants of his believing people. They ought to rest contented and happy in that assurance felt by David, " The Lord is my shepherd: I shall not want."—Moses reminded the Israelites of this, forty years afterwards. He says, " The Lord suffered thee to hunger." But then the Lord, after that they had endured hunger, supplied their need. Many are ready to cry out, when in want or pain, " Who is there to pity me?" Why, if thou art a believer in Christ, then Christ pities thee! You ask—" But why does he suffer me to hunger?" The answer is plain—To make thee look to Him more and more: to prove thy faith : and, most assuredly, to do thee good at thy latter end.

Yes, my friend; we are so used to the "daily bread" which God gives us, that we forget his power, his bounty, and his great patience towards us. Were it not for his goodness, the food we eat would give us no nourishment; and the medicine we sometimes take, would do us no good. Our life and health entirely depend on God's word, each moment. Oh, let us pray for faith in his love, and for thankfulness on the remembrance of his many mercies to us unworthy and perishing sinners.

5. Let me add a further observation on this miraculous supply.—How beautifully does this story remind us of our Lord Jesus Christ, who is *our* Manna. We read in St. John's Gospel, chapter vi. 48, that Jesus calls himself the Bread of Life.

The Jews had been talking and disputing with him, "saying, Our fathers did eat Manna in the desert;"—meaning thereby to ask, "And what miracle canst *thou* show?" Jesus immediately answers, "The bread of God is He which came down from heaven, and giveth life unto the world. I am the bread of life: he that cometh unto me shall never hunger; and he that believeth on me, shall never thirst."

My friend, seek to obtain a living faith in Christ, and let your soul feed on him, as your daily bread. Then will He be with you, by his Spirit, all through the wilderness of this world: and hereafter he will fill you with the treasures of the heavenly Canaan, treasures abundant and unfailing, for ever.

Some useful remarks might be made on other parts of this story:—especially, Observe the greediness with which some gathered for two days instead of one, and the way in which they were punished: their overplus putrified and stank. And so it is with those who heap up treasures for themselves, and are not rich towards God, nor bountiful to the poor:— their wealth is often their ruin and their shame, in the end.

Note also the disappointment of those, who went out to gather on the sabbath-day, "and found none." There is no blessing upon work done at forbidden times. The Lord's Day is to be sanctified. There are six days in which men ought to work: during these we may expect a blessing on the labour of our hands. Body and soul both need the holy rest of the Lord's Day.

But, in one word, let me exhort you—Live by faith in Christ! Then, all will go on well. Even if you suffer hardships, you are no worse off than Jesus was. Remember his words—" Foxes have holes, and birds of the air have nests; but the Son of Man hath not where to lay his head."

PRAYER.

O Lord God, the Creator and Preserver of all mankind: In thee we live, and move, and have our being. The eyes of all wait upon thee, and thou givest them their meat in due season. Cause us to feel our constant dependence on thee. Feed us with food convenient for us. When we have a sufficiency of all things, may we, with all moderation, use this world as not abusing it. If we are called to suffer adversity, lead us, as poor and needy and unworthy creatures, to cast all our care upon thee, who carest for us. Teach us, heavenly Father, in whatsoever state we are, therewith to be content.

Blessed be thou, O Lord, who dost never disappoint the souls that hunger and thirst after righteousness. In thy dear Son thou hast given unto us living bread, and waters of salvation that fail not. Blessed be thou, O Lord Jesu, who hast graciously condescended to offer unto us thy flesh, which is meat indeed; and thy blood, which is drink indeed. Blessed be thou, O Holy Spirit, who dost give life and power to the word of grace, and to all the ordinances of the Gospel, that by them the people of the Lord may be strengthened and refreshed, in their journeying through this great wilderness. Whatever want our bodies may suffer, Lord, let our souls be filled with the good things which minister unto salvation. Satisfy us with thy mercy in Christ. Evermore give us this Bread. Make us rich in faith, and heirs of the kingdom which thou hast promised to them that love thee, through Christ our Lord. Amen.

XVIII.
WATER FROM THE ROCK.
Exodus xvii. 1—7.

And all the congregation of the children of Israel journeyed from the wilderness of Sin, after their journeys, according to the commandment of the Lord, and pitched in Rephidim: and there was no water for the people to drink.

Wherefore the people did chide with Moses, and said, Give us water, that we may drink. And Moses said unto them, Why chide ye with me? wherefore do ye tempt the Lord?

And the people thirsted there for water; and the people murmured against Moses, and said, Wherefore is this, that thou hast brought us up out of Egypt, to kill us and our children and our cattle with thirst?

And Moses cried unto the Lord, saying, What shall I do unto this people? they be almost ready to stone me.

And the Lord said unto Moses, Go on before the people, and take with thee of the elders of Israel; and thy rod, wherewith thou smotest the river, take in thine hand, and go.

Behold, I will stand before thee there upon the rock in Horeb; and thou shalt smite the rock, and there shall come water out of it, that the people may drink. And Moses did so in the sight of the elders of Israel.

And he called the name of the place Massah, and Meribah, because of the chiding of the children of Israel, and because they tempted the Lord, saying, Is the Lord among us, or not?

ONE sign of a very evil heart is, when the heart cannot be softened by kindness. This is mournfully seen in the history of the Israelites. The Lord had been very kind to them, redeeming them out of Egypt, bringing them through the Red Sea, covering them with the pillar of a cloud, and feeding them with manna; and yet, the moment they suffered this new calamity, the want of water, they rebelled against Moses, being almost ready to stone him; and, what was still more criminal, they provoked the Lord to anger, crying out, with profane unbelief, " Is the Lord among us, or not?"

The forbearance and goodness of God on this occasion were wonderfully manifested. The Lord commanded Moses to go forth, with the elders of Israel, and to smite the rock in Horeb, with the rod which he had before used in smiting the river of Egypt. He did so; and God " brought streams out of the rock, and caused the waters to run down like rivers." " The waters gushed out, and the streams overflowed."

St. Paul, speaking of this event, says, " They did all drink of the same spiritual drink; for they drank of that rock which followed them, and that Rock was Christ:"—words, which prove that more was intended by this history, than the mere telling of a fact. That Rock, in truth, represented the abundant grace of our Lord Jesus Christ to perishing souls. In this view let us study the spiritual uses of the story : and may the Holy Spirit be our Teacher, and lead us to drink of those living waters which flow from Christ!

1. First, as the Israelites must all have died, if water had not been given them, so we, for our sins, must have perished eternally, if the goodness of God had not provided a supply of mercy for our souls.

Oh! that we were distressed by our dying state, as much as the Israelites were by their want of water! Natural thirst is quickly and most painfully felt: but sinners, languishing under the effects of sin, know nothing of their state, till convinced by the Holy Spirit of their guilt and wretchedness. It is one of the first proofs that a work of grace has been begun in the heart, when a sinner cries out, "I thirst—the world cannot satisfy me—my soul is athirst for the living God!"

2. When the misery of sin is felt, then let the eye of faith be directed to Christ, who is our smitten Rock. As one particular rock, that in Horeb, was especially mentioned by name; so likewise Christ Jesus was expressly appointed by God himself, to be our Source of grace. The supply of water from the rock was wholly unexpected:—in like manner, that grace should flow from our dying Redeemer, the Son of God, was a plan of mercy altogether beyond what could have been conceived of, by us, ignorant and ruined sinners.

3. The Israelites would crowd by thousands to

the waters gushing from the rock. Burning thirst led them; yea, compelled them. They would press, with their hands and lips, to the refreshing stream. It is *by faith* that the thirsting people of God come to Jesus for salvation. Faith shows them the sufficiency of his grace, and then leads them to Him. They are athirst: they are invited to the waters: by faith they accept the invitation: they drink, and live for ever.

4. And what is the grace, which, like a living stream, flows from Christ, our Rock? It is the gift of the Holy Spirit, bestowed on every one who asks for it in faith.—Various are the operations of the Spirit on the hearts of those who believe. Let us notice some of them.

—The Spirit leads us by faith to receive the doctrine of Christ's atonement. Thus, our sin is washed away: "The blood of Jesus Christ, the Son of God, cleanseth us from all sin."

—The Spirit purifies the soul from the defilement of sin, making our hearts holy, and filling them with grace. "If ye, through the Spirit, do mortify the deeds of the body, ye shall live." " A new heart will I give you, and a new spirit will I put within you: and I will take away the stony heart out of your flesh, and I will give you an heart of flesh. And I will put my Spirit within you, and cause you to walk in my statutes; and ye shall keep my judgments, and do them."

—As water makes the earth fruitful, so does the Spirit of Christ fertilize the soul. Without water from the rock, there would have been no grass for the cattle, no herb for the use of man in that dreary desert: so likewise, without the Spirit, we can bring forth no fruit:—as Jesus says, "Without me ye can do nothing." But the promise is, "I will pour water upon him that is thirsty, and floods upon the dry ground: I will pour my Spirit upon thy seed, and my blessing upon thine offspring. And they shall spring up as among the grass, as willows by the water-courses."

—Moreover, the Spirit of Christ animates, refreshes, and comforts the heart, as cool waters cheer the thirsty soul: therefore is the Holy Ghost called also "The Comforter." "When the poor and needy seek water, and there is none, and their tongue faileth for thirst, I the Lord will hear them. I the God of Israel will not forsake them. I will open rivers in high places, and fountains in the midst of the valleys."

—The streams of life and joy flowing from the Spirit of Christ are abundant and unfailing. "Whosoever," saith Christ, "drinketh of the water that I shall give him, shall never thirst: but the water that I shall give him, shall be in him a well of water, springing up into everlasting life."

You see, my friend, what cheering Gospel-truths lie hidden in the history of the Israelites. Hidden they are, to a careless eye: but they are plain to those who search the Scriptures with diligence and prayer. Let us, then, come to Christ, our Rock, our Well-spring, yea, our River of living water.

"With joy will we draw water out of the wells of salvation."

PRAYER.

O Lord Jesus Christ, who hast graciously promised to be with thy Church alway, even unto the end of the world: Pour down upon us, we beseech thee, the abundance of thy grace. Forgive our iniquities: pity our infirmities: confirm and strengthen us in every holy desire and purpose. Lord, increase our faith; and let us never doubt thy willingness to succour us in every trouble, and to bless us in all our ways.

Lord, think upon thy congregation, which thou hast purchased and redeemed of old. Send the plentiful rain of thy Holy Spirit, to refresh thine inheritance, when it is weary. Drop down, ye heavens, from above, and let the skies pour down righteousness. Let not any, O Lord, that wait on thee, go away ashamed: let the poor and needy praise thy name.

Guide us in peace through this great wilderness, and deliver us from all evil. Lead us at length to the Fountain of living waters above; even unto thy presence, where there is fulness of joy, and to thy right hand, where there are pleasures for evermore.

We ask these great mercies, for the sake of Jesus Christ, our Lord and our Redeemer. Amen.

XIX.

THE LAW:—THE FIRST TABLE.

Exodus xx. 1—11.

And God spake all these words, saying,

I am the Lord thy God, which have brought thee out of the land of Egypt, out of the house of bondage.

Thou shalt have no other gods before me.

Thou shalt not make unto thee any graven image, or any likeness of any thing that is in heaven above, or that is in the earth beneath, or that is in the water under the earth:

Thou shalt not bow down thyself to them, nor serve them: for I the Lord thy God am a jealous God, visiting the iniquity of the fathers upon the children unto the third and fourth generation of them that hate me;

And showing mercy unto thousands of them that love me, and keep my commandments.

Thou shalt not take the name of the Lord thy God in vain; for the Lord will not hold him guiltless that taketh his name in vain.

Remember the sabbath-day, to keep it holy.

Six days shalt thou labour, and do all thy work:

But the seventh day is the sabbath of the Lord thy God: in it thou shalt not do any work, thou, nor thy son, nor thy daughter, thy man-servant, nor thy maid-servant, nor thy cattle, nor thy stranger that is within thy gates:

For in six days the Lord made heaven and earth, the sea, and all that in them is, and rested the seventh day: wherefore the Lord blessed the sabbath-day, and hallowed it.

To know God, our Creator and Judge; to know that Law, according to which He will judge mankind at the Last Day;—and, moreover, to know and feel the power of the Gospel, by which our Redeemer shows mercy to repenting sinners;—this, my friend, is Man's truest wisdom. It is the study, of all others, most necessary for us. Let us, then, with humility and teachableness, hear what God the Lord hath spoken in the Ten Commandments. This Law belongs to us, as much as it did to the Israelites; and the right understanding of it prepares the heart for the right receiving of the Gospel. Let us then pray, like David, " Open thou mine eyes, that I may behold wondrous things out of thy law!"

It will be useful to explain each one of the Commandments, in its order.

1. The First Commandment forbids our having any other gods but the Lord Jehovah.

There is but one living and true God: his name is, Jehovah. He is the Creator, Upholder, and Governor of all things. All that we can see, or think of, excepting God, is created.

The Lord has revealed to us, that there are Three Persons in the Godhead; namely, the Father, the Son, and the Holy Ghost. They are not three Gods; but three Persons in one God. This God, and Him alone, we are to adore, to trust, to love, to serve, and to obey.

When it is said, " Thou shalt have no other gods," the expression pointedly condemns a sin which has been most awfully common in the world — the setting up of false gods. Thus, for example, the ancient Heathens worshipped Mars as the god of war, Minerva as the goddess of wisdom, and so forth. The Indians of the present day worship Juggernath, whose service is marked by cruelty and impurity. Men seem to have delighted in multiplying false gods. It was said of the Athenians of old, that in their superstitious city more gods were to be found than men: and the Hindoos are said to have three hundred and thirty-three millions of gods. Such are the inventions of fallen, sinful Man, blinded by Satan!

We despise these false gods: yet may there not also be gods *in the heart,* rivalling the True God, and taking away our affections from him? Certainly there may: and therefore let us not think, because we do not worship Jupiter or Mercury, that therefore we have never transgressed this commandment. The love of money is idolatry. Instead of trusting in God, who giveth us all things richly to enjoy, the worldly man says to gold, "*Thou* art my confidence." Some are lovers of pleasure, more than lovers of God: pleasure, then, is *their* idol: and agreeably to this, St. Paul says of the earthly-minded, "Whose god is their belly." Others make, as it were, a god of themselves: they say, "Who is lord over us?" They are proud of their Understanding. This is remarkably the case with Infidels: they idolize Human Reason, and set their own fancy higher than the word of God, and even against it. These men will sometimes profanely say, "There is no God:"—by which they mean in reality, that they will not have God to rule over them:—" in works, they deny him."

Yet further, the First Commandment is broken by all sorts of superstitious people; by those who pretend to have dealings with the Devil, by Fortune-tellers, Astrologers, and similar characters. For they forsake the True God, whose providence governs all things : and put faith in the stars, or in charms; or else in Fortune, or Luck, or Chance—unknown gods of man's inventing— from whom they teach their followers to expect some favour.

Others, again, worship Saints, and Angels, and the Blessed Virgin Mary, instead of God. They ask the Saints to pray God to have mercy on them; when they might approach God, and ought so to do, through Christ alone. They do not *call* the Saints, gods : but they worship them, and offer prayers to them; thus putting them in the place of God. They effectually set aside the doctrine, that Christ Jesus is our only Mediator. " No man," says Jesus, " cometh unto the Father, but by me." How, then, dare men come in any other way?

Again: Multitudes of men regard God, not as He has revealed Himself in the Bible, but according to their own imagination of Him. Some picture Him to their fancy as all Goodness; not taking into view his Justice, and his Hatred of sin. Others, on the contrary, deem Him all Justice and Holiness, despairing of his Mercy. Thus men set up one Attribute or Character of God, to the exclusion of the others. Some make a god, such as sinners need not fear : others, such a god, that desponding sinners can have no hope from him.

Thus you see, my friend, that the First Commandment forbids all false gods, all idols of the heart, all false religions, all superstitions, and all imperfect views of God. This command lies at the very foundation of all Religion. If we mistake here, we are wrong in every thing. We are to have no gods before the True God. If we set up any thing with Him, or in His place, it is setting Him aside. The True God, and a false god, cannot stand together. "The Lord our God is one Lord." " His glory will he not give to another."

2. The Second Commandment forbids the making of graven images and pictures for worship. Whether it be a pretended likeness of God the Father, or of Jesus Christ, or of the Holy Spirit, or of some saint, or angel, or false god, it is solemnly forbidden. For there is but One who ought to be worshipped, that is, God; and our worship of God is to be spiritual. "God is a Spirit; and they that worship him, must worship him in spirit and in truth."

What, then, mean the multitude of idols and images, before which men bow down, repeating their prayers, and kissing the carved, gilded, painted object of their devotions? All this, whether practised by Pagans or Papists, or by any other persons, is an abomination to God. Who that truly worships Him, as a Spirit, can need these idols of wood and stone? So far from helping us to worship aright,—which is the pretence often made for them,—idols and images do, in reality, draw away the heart *from* God. As soon as men begin to use any kind of idols, they begin to forsake God. And this is a sin which increases upon men: so that the second generation of idolaters necessarily proves worse than the first, and the third and fourth worse than the first and second. Thus increasing vengeance comes upon them from a jealous God: while He is abundantly good and gracious to those who practise and maintain spiritual worship.

For a particular account of idolatry, you may read Isaiah xliv. 12—20; and Acts xix. 23—41.

Perhaps you are ready to say, that you have never worshipped an image:—but if you are well satisfied with yourself simply on this account, it is very plain that you have not understood the spiritual sense of this commandment. Examine whether you have worshipped God as a Spirit. Let me put the following questions:—Do you in prayer constantly draw near to him by faith? Do you conscientiously walk as in His sight? Do you delight in praying to him? Do you habitually hold communion with him, through Jesus, by the Spirit? Or, do you trust in outward forms and observances; and are you ignorant—(entirely ignorant, or almost so)—of the power of godliness? These are searching questions: but without this self-examination you cannot know your real state.

3. The Third Commandment forbids perjury; or swearing that to be true which we know to be not so. It forbids, also, all profane and trifling use of the name of the Lord. "His name is great, wonderful and holy." We ought to address him

with the deepest reverence: and in conversation, we should never speak of him in a light and vain manner. False swearing by His name, is one of the greatest crimes a man can commit against society; and since false oaths may possibly escape being detected by man, therefore God declares that He will himself take the matter into his own hands:— for that is the force of the words, "The Lord will not hold him guiltless." As though He should say—A court of justice may fail to discover perjury; but God both can and will take vengeance on every false swearer: if not in this world, yet most certainly in the world to come.

Are you ready to say, that you have not broken this commandment;—or, at most, only now and then, and that slightly? Consider, that all irreverence about holy things is sin. If we make a jest of God's word, or of his service, or any of his people, we are guilty of taking God's name in vain. And surely you need not be told, that all kinds of common swearing—even what some persons consider to be small oaths, carelessly uttered without meaning—are a breach of this law. "Let your conversation be Yea, yea; Nay, nay: for whatsoever is more than these, cometh of evil."

4. The Fourth Commandment enjoins the religious observance of the Lord's Day. The seventh day was formerly the Sabbath, or day of rest; and it was kept in remembrance of the work of Creation. But, in honour of the far greater work of Man's Redemption, which was completed by the resur-

rection of Christ from the dead, God's Holy Day was changed from the seventh to the first day of the week. "This is the day which the Lord hath made: we will rejoice and be glad in it."

It is a proof of the goodness of God to Man, that he should thus have commanded one day in seven to be set apart as a day of holy rest. We need it for the well-being both of body and soul: and it is a blessed means of preparation for that heavenly rest, which remaineth for the people of God.

Especially, we ought to observe this holy day in honour of our God and Saviour. United Public Worship could not have been universally established in the world, if a general day of rest had not been fixed for it: and if the appointment had not been made by God himself, men would never have found any way of coming to an agreement among themselves. Whereas now, not only a whole nation, but even the whole world, may, within the period of the same twenty-four hours, publicly adore the Living and True God, and his Son Jesus Christ.

How grievously, then, do men sin against God—against their own souls, against their family, their children, and their neighbours—by profaning the Lord's Day! Worldly pleasures or work, idleness, visiting, and travelling, are destructive of the holy rest of God's own blessed day. He has indeed allowed works of necessity, and works of mercy, to be done on this day: but none else. Consider well, my friend, how *you* have spent the many sabbaths that have been granted to you during your life!

Let me add, that our Lord Jesus Christ has summed up this first part of the Law in the following words:—" Thou shalt love the Lord thy God with all thy heart, and with all thy soul, and with all thy mind, and with all thy strength: this is the first and great commandment."—It is time now to close these remarks with humble prayer.

PRAYER.

Holy, holy, holy Lord God of Hosts! Father, Son and Holy Ghost, three Persons in one God! We, thy unworthy creatures, fall down before the throne of thy Majesty, humbling ourselves for our innumerable sins, negligences and ignorances; yet hoping in thy mercy. Thou art a just God, and a Saviour. Thou wilt by no means clear the guilty, who walk on still in darkness, after their hardness and impenitent heart: but thou art full of compassion and goodness to them that fear thee, and that walk before thee in truth. Lord, help us to come to thee with humble, believing hearts. We confess, with shame, that other lords, beside thee, have had dominion over us: but by thee only we would now make mention of thy Name.

Teach us, Heavenly Father, by thine enlightening Spirit, to know thee, the only true God, and Jesus Christ whom thou hast sent, which is life eternal. Impress us with godly fear; and endue us with that spiritual mind, which thou requirest of them that worship thee. Incline our hearts to wait on thee, in the duties of meditation, prayer and praise. Bless to us the reading of thy word, and the use of thy divine ordinances. Especially dispose us to hallow thy sabbaths, and to worship thee with a pure worship; and fill us with joy when we go up to thine house, with the multitude of them that keep that holy day.

Keep us from profaneness, and from every false way. Suffer us not to forget that thine eye is ever upon us, and that thou, most upright, dost try the hearts of the children of men. We believe that thou wilt come to be our Judge: O let us be found of thee in peace, being accepted in Jesus, and made meet for the inheritance of the saints in light.

Lord, let thy way be known upon earth, thy saving health among all nations. Put an end to all idolatry and superstition, all error, impiety, and infidelity. Let the heathen fear the name of the Lord, and all the kings of the earth thy glory. Purify thy Church, and make it a blessing to all the nations of mankind. Hasten the time when all families shall be blessed, in Christ our exalted Redeemer; when every tongue shall confess to him, saying, The Lord is our Judge; the Lord is our Lawgiver; the Lord is our King: he will save us.

We ask these great mercies, for ourselves and for others, in the name of Jesus Christ our Lord: to whom, with the Father and the Holy Ghost, be glory in the Church, throughout all ages, world without end. Amen.

XX.

THE LAW:—THE SECOND TABLE.

Exodus xx. 12—17.

Honour thy father and thy mother: that thy days may be long upon the land which the Lord thy God giveth thee.

Thou shalt not kill.

Thou shalt not commit adultery.

Thou shalt not steal.

Thou shalt not bear false witness against thy neighbour.

Thou shalt not covet thy neighbour's house, thou shalt not covet thy neighbour's wife, nor his man-servant, nor his maid-servant, nor his ox, nor his ass, nor any thing that is thy neighbour's.

We have considered the First Table of the Law. In proceeding to the Second, let us remember how our Saviour has summed it up in one short sentence: "Thou shalt love thy neighbour as thyself." Simple as the words are, Jesus has made them, if possible, yet more clear by the following precept: "Whatsoever ye would that men should do to you, do ye even so to them." St. Paul likewise remarks, "Love worketh no ill to his neighbour: therefore love is the fulfilling of the law."

To the great question "Who is my neighbour?"—we find our Lord's answer, in Luke x. 29—37.

5. The Fifth Commandment is designed to enforce the duties which men owe one to another, in the different relations of society.

Although the relation of children to parents, which is the highest after that of man and wife, is the one here mentioned; yet every member of the family, and also friends, neighbours, fellow-countrymen, fellow-creatures—all, without exception, are comprehended in the general design of this law.

"Honour thy father and thy mother." That is, reverence them; love them; obey them in all things lawful; comfort and help them, when sick, poor, or aged: if they fear and worship God, have a special regard for them: if, unhappily, they live an irreligious life, never expose their faults needlessly; do not provoke them; endeavour to do them good; and constantly pray to God for them.

It would be impossible, in a short compass, to speak of all the duties of parents—of neighbours—of rulers and subjects — of ministers and their flocks. They are briefly summed up in the words, "Honour all men." As far as possible, let us be respectful, kind, dutiful, serviceable to all, and at peace with all: and let us be clothed with humility.

A special promise is added to this commandment: to those who keep it, happiness, even in this world, is promised. Those persons who endeavour the most extensively to be a blessing to others shall be the most largely blessed themselves.

6. The Sixth Commandment forbids Murder. But it condemns, not that horrid crime alone, but also all the passions that lead to it. It forbids all anger, strife, and clamour—all violence and fighting—all sullenness, resentment, hatred, and ill-will—an unforgiving spirit—bitter and provoking words—all harshness, cruelty, and unkindness. St. John

says, " He that hateth his brother is a murderer."
—Take a common example: the child that quarrels with his play-fellows does, in spirit, break this law. The seed of murder is in his little breast.

7. The Seventh Commandment forbids not only that great crime which is named in it; but all sins of the same character and tendency; that is, all kinds of Impurity, whether in action, or in word, thought, or even look. Our Lord has thus explained this commandment: " Whosoever looketh on a woman to lust after her, hath committed adultery with her already in his heart."

On the same principle, all Intemperance, Gluttony, Sloth, and sinful indulgence of the carnal appetites, are forbidden. Temperance, Sobriety, and Chastity, are duties which we owe alike to God, to ourselves, and to society at large.

8. The Eighth Commandment forbids Stealing. With equal force it condemns all sorts of dishonesty, cheating in trade, and over-reaching of our neighbours in bargains. " A false balance is an abomination unto the Lord: but a just weight is his delight."—Mis-spending of other people's time is a very common breach of this law.

9. The Ninth Commandment forbids bearing False Witness against our Neighbour. Can we conceive a greater cruelty, than to take away the good name, the property, or possibly the life, of a fellow-creature, by a deliberate lie! Could we be content that others should do so to us? This command forbids every kind of calumny and

deceit. Not only does the law of love forbid false accusations; but it restrains the needless talking about the faults of others. How sore are we, when others speak against *us!* How backward then ought we to be, in speaking against others! Tattlers, whisperers, backbiters, gossips, and busy-bodies in other men's matters, break this law continually.

When we consider how spiritual the law of God is, how can we refrain from crying out with David, " Who can understand his errors? Cleanse thou me from secret faults!"

10. But if we would understand the length, and breadth, and depth of the Divine Law, we must study well the Tenth Commandment, " Thou shalt not covet." Several things are mentioned, which are apt to excite our covetous or envious passions; such as our neighbour's property, or the pleasing and desirable circumstances of his family and connections. When we see a person happy in the possession of something which we have not, the throught springs up naturally in our wicked hearts —" Oh, I wish I had that!" And we are so selfish, that we wish it out of our neighbour's possession, into our own hands. Self, from first to last, is the idol of our hearts. We may learn the art of keeping many of our evil thoughts to ourselves: but there they all are—in the heart! Children have not so well acquired the art of concealing: and therefore they covet and beg and snatch, all in the same moment. But every man, who carefully observes his heart, perceives that the

passions of coveting, longing, envying, &c. are natural to him. And nothing but Divine Grace can root them out, and keep the soul at rest, surrounded as we are in this evil world by so many objects of desire.

Now it is this movement of the soul, called Coveting, which especially tends to prove the wickedness and depravity of man. St. Paul remarks, "I had not known lust, except the Law had said, Thou shalt not covet." This one commandment, yea, this single opening sentence of it, "Thou shalt not covet," showed to the Apostle, in the strongest light, the excessive vileness of his heart. "For the word of God is quick and powerful, and sharper than any two-edged sword;—it is a discerner of the thoughts and intents of the heart." Men can judge only by what is outward: but God's law deals with the thoughts and feelings, with the imagination, the wishes, and the purposes of every man. And thus it is that Conscience condemns us all. Each one, for the sins of his heart as well as those of his life, must plead guilty before God.

Some may say, "What harm do I do to my neighbour, by merely longing for a thing which he has, and I have not?" Let me answer, by putting two or three other questions:—Do you not secretly repine at your own lot;—and is not this rebellion against God's Providence? Do you put out your whole strength to do the best you can for yourself? If not, is not this indolence? Idle persons are, of all others, the most ready to indulge discontent and envy. Are you not sometimes inclined to lay your hand on your neighbour's property? If so, do you see no evil in first wishing and hankering after it? Alas! this single fact of your coveting and longing—or, as Scripture calls it, this " evil concupiscence"—this is the very seed of sin. Yea, it is itself sin. " For," as our Lord Jesus Christ says, " from within, out of the heart of men, proceed evil thoughts, adulteries, fornications, murders, thefts, covetousness, wickedness, deceit, lasciviousness, an evil eye, blasphemy, pride, foolishness: all these evil things come from within, and defile the man."

Abundant matter is thus set before us, my friend, for humiliation, confession, and prayer. Let us, at some other opportunity, consider how greatly we need the pardoning mercy of our God, and the grace of his sanctifying Spirit; all which may be fully learned from the Gospel.

PRAYER.

O Lord God, who hast so loved the world as to give thine only-begotten Son, that whosoever believeth in him should not perish, but have everlasting life. Fill our hearts, we pray thee, with that spirit of pity, goodness, and love, which thou hast thyself manifested toward the children of men.

Thou only, O Lord, art able to heal the diseases of our souls, and to quiet the disorders of this sinful world. For ourselves, we must with shame confess, that we are naturally such as thy word declares us to be—children of wrath, foolish, disobedient, deceived, serving divers lusts and pleasures, living in malice and envy, hateful and hating one another. Oh, how great is thy condescension, that thou shouldest look upon such creatures as we are! But we entreat thee, Lord, not only to pardon all our sins, but also to shed on us abundantly the renewing grace of thy Holy Spirit. Cause the fruit of thy Spirit to spring forth in our hearts and lives; in love, joy, peace, long-suffering, gentleness, goodness, faith, meekness, temperance. Dispose and enable us to love Thee above all things; and to love one another with a pure heart, fervently.

We beseech thee to bestow on us those family blessings and comforts, of which thou knowest us to stand in need. Especially, we pray that our dear relatives and friends may be brought into the household of faith. O remove far from us every evil way. Mortify in us all corrupt affections, all pride and selfishness, all sensuality and covetousness, all unkindness and hardness of heart. Make us dutiful and loving, gentle and easy to be entreated, pure and temperate, diligent and faithful, honest and disinterested in our dealings with all men. Dispose us to be kind one to another, tender-hearted, forgiving one another, even as God for Christ's sake hath forgiven us.

Have compassion, O Lord, on the poor, the afflicted, the infirm, the sick, and the aged. Incline our hearts to do them good: and may we give, not grudgingly, but cheerfully, knowing that we are stewards of the Lord on their behalf. Show pity to all that are persecuted or oppressed. Put an end to slavery, and cruelty of every kind. Hasten the blessed time when nation shall not rise up against nation, neither shall they learn war any more. Let the whole earth be filled with thy glory, for thy dear Son's sake, Jesus Christ our Lord. Amen, and Amen.

XXI.

THE LAW, AND THE GOSPEL.

Exodus xx. 18—21.

And all the people saw the thunderings, and the lightnings, and the noise of the trumpet, and the mountain smoking: and when the people saw it, they removed, and stood afar off.

And they said unto Moses, Speak thou with us, and we will hear: but let not God speak with us, lest we die.

And Moses said unto the people, Fear not: for God is come to prove you, and that his fear may be before your faces, that ye sin not.

And the people stood afar off, and Moses drew near unto the thick darkness where God was.

THE terror, which the Israelites felt at the giving of the Law, was natural and just. Conceive hundreds of thousands of men, women, and children, standing round the foot of an immense mountain, the upper part of which was altogether in a smoke, while the Lord descended upon it in fire. The sky, far and wide, was filled with thunder and lightning, while the voice of a trumpet—fit expression of the majesty of God's Law—sounded long, and gradually waxed louder and louder. The people, hearing and seeing all this, and feeling the shocks which made the mountain quake to its very base, trembled exceedingly, and removed and stood afar off.

In their feelings and conduct, we see a lively emblem of the terrors of the law moving a guilty conscience. As the Israelites then felt, so ought we to feel, when we consider the holiness of the God with whom we have to do, and our own utter sinfulness, helplessness, and unworthiness to appear before Him. When conscience is awakened, we, like the Israelites, shall stand far off from the Law: we shall cry to our Mediator, Christ Jesus, of whom Moses was a type: and our earnest supplication to Jesus will be like theirs—" Speak Thou unto us: speak in words of mercy and reconciliation: let not the sentence of the Law take effect upon our souls, lest we die."

Suffer me to lay before you, my friend, a few remarks concerning the Law, and the Gospel; in the hope that you may be led to flee to that Saviour, who alone can deliver us from the wrath to come.

1. First observe, that the Ten Commandments are addressed to us, individually. "*Thou* shalt—*Thou* shalt not." For, while the Law of God is given to thousands and millions, yet each man is as much concerned, as if the whole Law were given to him alone. God is the Judge of all; "but every one of us shall give account of *himself* to God."

2. Next, remark how the Commandments are given in the language of *forbidding*—" Thou *shalt not.*" What does this show, but that we are all naturally inclined to sin? When a parent says to his child, " You must not do this or that," it is because he knows what his child is disposed to do, what his other children have already done, and cousequently what any one of them is likely to do again. Thus it is with our Heavenly Father—he knows that "the imagination of man's heart is only evil from his youth:" he sees that our first bent is, to depart from Him and holiness. Therefore it is that the word " Not" is used so often.

3. Consider, next, what an awful mass of sin and corruption does the Law detect in our hearts and lives! " By the Law is the knowledge of sin." The Law, by displaying the perfect holiness of God, shows us our own guilt. Thus it appears that "all have sinned, and come short of the glory of God." In our childhood, in our youth, in our manhood, we have never been without sin! In much of our lives has there not been abounding iniquity? For remember, that, in examining ourselves, we are to include sins of the heart, as well as sins of action; our tempers and our words, as well as our conduct; omissions, as well as sins actually committed. Read again the explanations of the First Commandment, and of the Tenth; and you will see how great and numerous are our sins of omission, and the sins of our hearts. The not knowing God, not seeking to know Him, the not liking to retain

God in our knowledge, the natural springing up of evil imaginations, the disposition to cherish them, the bad thought, though followed by no bad action —all these things, in God's sight, are sins.

4. The Law, therefore, condemns us. For it is written, " Cursed is every one that continueth not in all things which are written in the book of the Law to do them." And again, " Whosoever shall keep the whole law, and yet offend in one point, he is guilty of all.— For he that said, Do not commit adultery, said also, Do not kill. Now, if thou commit no adultery, yet if thou kill, thou art become a transgressor of the law." As the Israelites therefore trembled, expecting nothing less than death, as even Moses said, "I exceedingly fear and quake;"—so should Conscience fill us with terror, to think that judgment is ready to fall upon us—*except we repent!*

5. But let us turn from these terrors of the Law, to the hopes and consolations of the Gospel. " Christ hath redeemed us from the curse of the law, being made a curse for us." Under the Gospel Covenant, " To him that worketh not, but believeth in him that justifieth the ungodly, his faith is counted for righteousness." We cannot be saved by our works: by faith we may, and shall be, saved. O then come with humble confidence to Christ. Ask for a full pardon, through his most precious blood. In him, be reconciled unto God. Being justified by faith, you may have peace. Fear not; ye shall not die. For though Conscience

accuses, and the Law condemns, yet "we have an Advocate with the Father, Jesus Christ the righteous; and He is the propitiation for our sins." Christ died for us: Christ pleads for us: Christ speaks to us: his words are full of comfort—"Believe, and live." "The law was given by Moses; but grace and truth came by Jesus Christ."

6. "Shall we then continue in sin?" What! because grace forgives and blots out all the past, shall we act as if our reconciled Father did not require holiness from us? God forbid!—The Gospel, which alone gives us hope, enjoins also the most hearty, the most spiritual obedience to God. "Having therefore these promises, dearly beloved, let us cleanse ourselves from all filthiness of the flesh and spirit, perfecting holiness in the fear of God." God requires, "that his fear should be before our faces, that we sin not." The fear spoken of, is such as loving children feel. "This is the love of God, that we keep his commandments: and his commandments are not grievous." And the Lord offers us effectual help, even the help of his Holy Spirit, that we may be enabled to please Him, in thought, word, and deed. Believers in Christ are the only persons that truly practise holiness: for they are created anew in Christ: their life springs from Christ, to whom they are united as members of the body to the head. The law of love is stamped upon their heart. They possess that "faith which worketh by love."

May this living union with Christ be ours, manifested by the abundant fruits of righteousness: and thus may grace, mercy and peace flow to us, from God the Father, and Christ Jesus our Lord!

PRAYER.

O thou high and lofty One, that inhabitest Eternity, whose name is Holy: Thou art greatly to be feared, and to be had in reverence of all that are round about thee. If even Angels veil their faces in thy presence, who and what are we, that we should approach the throne of thy Divine Majesty? Lord, we are not worthy to take thy name within our lips. We must cry, Unclean! unclean! When we meditate on thy purity, thy hatred of sin, and thine almighty power, we are constrained every one of us to say, Woe is me, for I am undone! Lord, we humble ourselves before thee: we abhor ourselves, and repent in dust and ashes.

Blessed, for ever blessed, be thy Name, that thou hast provided a way, by which the most unworthy may come to thee. In Jesus thou art ready to pardon and accept the guilty. Thou layest aside all thy wrath, and showest a countenance full of love and kindness to him that is poor and of a contrite spirit, and that trembleth at thy word. O Heavenly Father, we now draw nigh unto thee, through Jesus, the Mediator of the New Covenant. Receive us graciously: grant us pardon and peace: bless us, in turning away every one of us from our iniquities.

Incline our hearts unto thy testimonies, and quicken us in thy ways. Let thy Holy Spirit dwell in us, and walk in us; stirring up holy affections, and strengthening us daily, more and more, for thy service. Put thy fear within us, that we may be kept from sinning against thee. Order our footsteps by thy word: so shall no iniquity have dominion over us. Keep us from falling; and, finally, present us faultless before the presence of thy glory, with exceeding joy, through Jesus Christ, our Mediator and Advocate. Amen.

XXII.

THE FIERY SERPENTS.

Numbers xxi. 5—9.

And the people spake against God, and against Moses, Wherefore have ye brought us up out of Egypt, to die in the wilderness? for there is no bread, neither is there any water; and our soul loatheth this light bread.

And the Lord sent fiery serpents among the people, and they bit the people; and much people of Israel died.

Therefore the people came to Moses, and said, We have sinned, for we have spoken against the Lord, and against thee: pray unto the Lord that he may take away the serpents from us. And Moses prayed for the people.

And the Lord said unto Moses, Make thee a fiery serpent, and set it upon a pole: and it shall come to pass, that every one that is bitten, when he looketh upon it, shall live.

And Moses made a serpent of brass, and put it upon a pole: and it came to pass, that if a serpent had bitten any man, when he beheld the serpent of brass, he lived.

This would be a very instructive story, if considered only by itself; but our Lord Jesus Christ has shown us, that it is also a lively picture of the evil of sin, and of the sufficiency of that salvation which he purchased for us, when he died upon the cross.

The bite of sin is more dreadful than the bite of fiery serpents; for it poisons the soul. All mankind are suffering from it. It is the bite of that old serpent, the devil. See how fiercely it inflames the soul with raging lusts, which hurry men on into perdition! Some men, even in this life, seem to be almost in hell—swearing, fighting, lying, drinking, gambling, stealing; running into all sorts of riot and excess; speaking against God; vexing the hearts of the godly; jesting about the devil; and madly sporting on the very brink of ruin! These are of their father the devil; they do the works of their father; and, except they repent, they will at last have their portion with the devil and his angels, in the lake that burneth with fire and brimstone.

But there are sinners of another kind—men who outwardly appear decent before men, but whose hearts are full of evil in the sight of God. Solomon speaks of such, when he says, "There is a generation that are pure in their own eyes, and yet are not washed from their filthiness." Such are, the proud; the covetous; those who attend public worship from custom only; those who go about to establish their own righteousness, thinking they need no better; and who will not accept that perfect righteousness, the righteousness which is of God by faith. In all such persons, sin is working like a slow poison. It does not show itself, so as to alarm them: still, they are most surely dying, from the venomous sting of sin.

Every thing that falls short of perfect love to God, and perfect love to man, is sin: so, then, all are sinners, and all have come short of the glory of God.

The remedy for sin is simple, being Faith in Christ. Jesus himself explained this to Nicodemus, when he said, "And, as Moses lifted up the serpent in the wilderness, even so must the Son of Man be lifted up, that whosoever believeth in him should not perish, but have everlasting life."

Who would have thought that a brazen serpent, set up on a pole, could do any good to persons bitten by fiery serpents? Some would have said, "Put a plaster upon the wound; or pour into it some healing ointment." But God had appointed another way—one only way. And they who looked at the brazen serpent were healed, because they believed His word.

Thus we direct dying sinners to Christ crucified. It is vain to tell them, "Try to do your best;" for men cannot save themselves. We must say to sinners, as Christ did, "God so loved the world, that he gave his only-begotten Son, that whosoever believeth in him should not perish, but have everlasting life." Therefore, O sinners, believe in Him.

Let me ask, Have *you* felt the misery of your sins? Are you looking for a cure to the Lord Jesus Christ alone? When you hear of His saving name, do you turn the eye of faith towards Him? And as faith and hope increase, do love and joy spring up in your heart, so that you are ready to sing, "Unto Him that loved us, and washed us from our sins in his own blood, to him be praise and dominion for ever!"

Or, are you one of those who think that sin is not so deadly in you, as in some of your neighbours; that, as you have done nobody any harm, you have no great need of a Saviour; for, after all, you have a good heart?. 'Alas! I must tell you, that you are greatly deceived. If you knew the real case, you would find that your heart is the worst thing about you. Thousands of evil thoughts have lodged in it. It is deceitful above all things, and desperately wicked. It needs to be wholly changed. You ought to pray, without ceasing—"Pardon all my sins, in heart and life; and create in me a clean heart, O God, for Christ's sake!"

There are some who will say, "Tell me no more of Christ: I am so far gone in sin, that I cannot repent: let me die as I am!"—But I ask, "Why will you die?" Answer me that one question, "Why?" Think of it day and night.—Why will you not live? Why will you not believe? Why will you not cast a look toward Christ? Why will you not pray for faith in him?—Think of a man dying in agonies, from the bite of a serpent: yet, just at the point of death, if he would but look at the brazen serpent, he lived. So, if you would only look to Christ with faith, you would have pardon for all the past: you would pass from death unto life; and be made a new creature in Christ Jesus. With such a Saviour, then, set before your eyes, why will you die?

PRAYER.

O Lord, who is a God like unto thee, that pardonest iniquity, transgression, and sin? Thou retainest not thine anger for ever, because thou delightest in mercy. O turn again, and have compassion upon us! Subdue our iniquities: cast all our sins behind thy back. Quicken us, by thy good Spirit, in our approaches to thee, that we may come in an acceptable time. To-day, while it is called to-day, we make haste to seek thee: let not our hearts become hardened, through the deceitfulness of sin.

Turn thou us, good Lord, and so we shall be turned. Draw us, and we will run after thee. Heal our souls, for we have sinned against thee. Take away all iniquity; receive us graciously and love us freely, for thy dear Son's sake, Jesus Christ our Lord. Amen.

XXIII.

THIS GREAT WILDERNESS.

Deuteronomy ii. 7.

He knoweth thy walking through this great wilderness.

The goodness of God to his people is continually spoken of in Scripture: and it was remarkably shown in his care of the Israelites during their forty years' sojourn in the wilderness.

We may consider this journeying of the children of Israel through the wilderness as a picture of our Christian pilgrimage through the world. At every step, the Lord knoweth our walking, as he knew theirs. In our course, therefore, we should implore the loving-kindness of God. " The Lord knoweth them that are his:"—and He will keep them, even unto the end.

May his Spirit instruct us, while we are considering this comfortable doctrine—that, if we be his true servants, then his eye is always over us, for our good!

Observe in how many respects the Lord watches over his faithful people.

1. First, the Lord knoweth our Entering upon the Christian pilgrimage. He knows the time of our conversion, and all the circumstances of it. The first entrance upon our Christian walk is marked by a mighty deliverance. As the Israelites were brought out of the land of Egypt, out of the house of bondage, so believers in Christ are brought out of the slavery of sin and Satan, and delivered from this present evil world.

Think, then, my friend, whether you have taken the first step in your journey to the heavenly Canaan. Have you believed and obeyed the call of your Redeemer? Have you repented of sin, and endeavoured to shake off its yoke? Have you sought pardon through Christ; and do you desire to be his willing servant? Have you left the broad road that leadeth to destruction, and given up worldly and vain company? How were you led to this blessed change? The Lord knows all the circumstances; but it is well for you also to remember them, so far as you possibly can. Perhaps you were led on gently, in the course of Christian education. Or, can you tell what sermon it was—what minister or parent or friend—or what affliction, or what book—that first led you to think seriously? If you can, meditate most thankfully on all these particulars. Blessed time! when you began your pilgrimage heavenward; when you turned your back on a sinful world, having your heart touched with the love of Christ!

2. Moreover, the Lord knoweth our Wants in this great wilderness, after we have entered upon it.—The children of Israel at one season wanted food; and at another time, water: and do not our souls continually need grace? The wilderness furnished no supplies: in like manner, the world can give us no help in serving God. Our own corrupt hearts help us not. The grace which we need must be given us from above. St. Paul, speaking on this subject, remarks—" They drank of that spiritual Rock, which followed them: and that Rock was Christ." Yes, my friend; Christ is the manna offered to every hungering soul: Christ is the living water, freely given to the thirsty.

3. The Lord also knows our Trials. "Many are the afflictions of the righteous: but the Lord delivereth him out of them all." The pathway in the wilderness is not smooth and even: it is very

rough, steep, and winding. There are many enemies by the way; many spiritual enemies, that war against the soul. All the temptations and trials that we meet with, may be compared to those bitter enemies, or to those fiery serpents and scorpions, which the Israelites encountered. The Lord knows what dangers we have to pass through: but mark his promise:—" There hath no temptation taken you, but such as is common to man: but God is faithful, who will not suffer you to be tempted above that ye are able; but will with the temptation also make a way to escape, that ye may be able to bear it."

4. The Lord knoweth also the Backslidings of his people. What an humbling thought! Our wanderings by the way, how many have they been! For though his grace is always sufficient for us, yet we do not always seek for it, or walk according to it. Observe the conduct of Israel in the wilderness: scarcely had they begun their journeyings, when they turned and provoked the Lord to anger; and, in various degrees, this was their behaviour all their journey through. What a picture of *our* hearts! If we know any thing of ourselves, we must confess with shame, that sometimes we have been weary of God's service; at other times we have quite turned from it: now we have wished to go back to Egypt; that is, to the world and sin; at another time we have been vexed, because God punished and corrected us. Oh, what a sad spectacle is the very best man's heart, when he faithfully

looks into it! And if to ourselves we appear such wanderers, what must we appear in the sight of God!

5. Yet the Lord knoweth also our Victories: for it is He himself who gives them to us. Sin, though it may sorely beset a believer, shall not have dominion over him. No;—by God's grace he fights manfully, and he fights successfully. God sees him in the midst of the battle, and gives him strength to fight. Many a victory does he gain in secret, while praying in his closet. In fact, without prayer he cannot fight and conquer. Pray, therefore: "continue instant in prayer:" "pray without ceasing:" persevere, as Moses did, (Exod. xvii. 9—15); and then you shall say, like him, "The Lord is my banner."

6. Let me add this only, that the Lord knoweth the End of our "walking in this great wilderness." This is something beyond the present moment: life will soon come to an end, and yet "man knoweth not his time." We may all say, like Isaac—"I know not the day of my death." But it is known to the Lord: and He will order all its circumstances, wisely and mercifully, if we walk closely with Him. Therefore, let us trust in Jesus as our Saviour: let us pray to be led by his good Spirit, and kept faithful to him, with the promised crown of glory full in view.

Take the comfort of these words—"This God is our God for ever and ever: he will be our guide, even unto death."

DEUTERONOMY II. 7.

PRAYER.

O Almighty God, who art the Guide and Comforter of all thy people : Lead us, we beseech thee, by the counsels of thy word, and by the inspiration of thy Holy Spirit, through all the trials of this changing life; and enable us to glorify thee by patient continuance in well-doing. Forgive us, good Lord, our multiplied rebellions against thee. Heal our backslidings. Turn us again; and dispose us with a true heart to follow thy commands, and to walk in thy paths.

Of thy bountiful providence, give what thou seest to be good for us: and supply all our spiritual wants out of the riches of thy grace in Christ Jesus. Grant us the comfort of thy presence, and the light of thy countenance, to support us in all our tribulations. Carry us safely through all temptations. Suffer not the enemy to prevail against us; and let not sin have dominion over us. And finally do thou receive us into those eternal mansions, which are prepared for all them that love and serve thee, through Jesus Christ, our Mediator and Redeemer. Amen.

XXIV.

REVIEW OF LIFE.

Deuteronomy viii. 2—5.

And thou shalt remember all the way which the Lord thy God led thee these forty years in the wilderness, to humble thee, and to prove thee, to know what was in thine heart, whether thou wouldest keep his commandments, or no.

And he humbled thee, and suffered thee to hunger, and fe

thee with manna, which thou knewest not, neither did thy fathers know; that he might make thee know that man doth not live by bread only, but by every word that proceedeth out of the mouth of the Lord doth man live.

Thy raiment waxed not old upon thee, neither did thy foot swell, these forty years.

Thou shalt also consider in thine heart, that, as a man chasteneth his son, so the Lord thy God chasteneth thee.

It is needful very often to stir up our hearts with that word, "Remember": or, as Moses says more pointedly in another passage—"Remember, and forget not."

Let us reflect on the lessons taught us by this affecting command to the Israelites: and may the Spirit of God be our Teacher, that we may profit by the present meditation!

Observe, that the command is, to "Remember *all* the way." Possibly this may appear a long task. To the aged it must be so; and to all of us it is a difficult undertaking, to review the whole of life. The best plan is—to divide our life into parts, noting the chief events of each part. Think of every remarkable event in your life—private; domestic; public—good, or evil—concerning your body, or your soul. The more closely you think, the more exactly you will remember.—And, entreat God to revive your memory, for this holy purpose.

A quiet hour by ourselves on the Lord's Day is an excellent season for these recollections.

This is also a very suitable subject for a Birthday meditation.

1. The first lesson which we should learn is, the

doctrine of God's over-ruling Providence. Life is called, " the way which *the Lord thy God* hath led thee."

Look at all the way, and see how He has led you in it. We often fancy that we are choosers of our own path: but in this we are entirely mistaken: it is the Lord who conducts us. We are led by an Unseen Hand. " There are many devices in a man's heart: nevertheless, the counsel of the Lord, that shall stand." Our life, from first to last, is subject to his providence. Has he not often led you by a way that you knew not? Has he not led you more wisely than you could have guided yourself? Has he not again and again made " crooked things straight, and darkness light, before you ?"

2. There are great lessons also to be learned from that Discipline, by which the Lord tries his people. Especially he designs to teach them Self-Humiliation, and to make them feel their entire dependence on Him.

We may see, on reviewing life, many chastenings that we have been called to endure. The Lord suffers his children to hunger—to fall sick—to be tried by poverty, by the unkindness of Man, and by many other troubles. In all this, he has wise and kind purposes. He deals with us, as a father with the son that he tenderly loves. He intends "to prove us;" to see whether we will follow him fully, or obey him only when his way pleases us —whether we will bear the reproach of Christ— whether we serve him from love, or from self-interest—in a word, whether or not we are his faithful people.

And can it be that this Discipline has failed of discovering to us the evil of our hearts? Affliction, it is true, hardens ungodly men: but it softens a child of God into the tenderest grief, on account his manifold corruptions.

What a blessed effect is this! When a loving disciple of Christ reviews his past course, he is deeply reminded of his own unworthiness. Occasionally, as he remembers particular seasons of his life, he cannot help crying out, "O my God, I am ashamed, and blush to lift up my face unto thee, my God!" He remembers wherein he has sinned; how he has grieved the Holy Spirit; how often he has trifled with conscience; how negligent of prayer he has been; how scanty in good works. He wonders that he has been kept in the way of salvation. He is convinced, in his own case at least, that "the righteous scarcely are saved." Again and again he cries out, "O blessed Jesu, mine was all the guilt and shame: the grace hath been wholly Thine, and to Thee be all the praise!"

Looking back on past days, how continually are we also reminded of our Dependence on God.— "He fed thee with manna." He kept thy raiment from waxing old, and thy foot from swelling. These were miraculous exertions of his power.—But the same almighty goodness is daily manifested to us in the bread we eat, in the raiment that covers us, and in the innumerable temporal blessings we enjoy.

For health, safety, well-being, and life itself, we must look entirely to God.—And for the higher blessings needed by our souls, do we not depend altogether on his free grace? Where can a lost sinner find rest, but in the merits of the Redeemer? Can we make to ourselves one crumb of spiritual food, can we find one drop of spiritual comfort, without Jesus? Impossible! He himself tells us, " Without me ye can do nothing."

3. There is yet another lesson to be drawn from the review of life; and it is one of a cheering kind. It is, the duty of mingled Thankfulness and Hope.

This we may learn from an expression used in a later verse of this chapter (ver. 16): " That he might humble thee, and that he might prove thee, *to do thee good at thy latter end.*"

Consider the goodness and mercy which thus far have followed you. Compare your case with that of others.—It is deeply affecting to remember what numbers of our early companions have been summoned to death and judgment, while we are yet alive!—An Israelite, looking back through those forty years, could remember many such cases: some cut off for murmuring; others for lusting after evil things; others swallowed up by an earthquake, for their rebellion; a man stoned to death for sabbath-breaking; the two sons of Aaron struck dead, for profaneness; and various other grievous judgments. Cannot we, too, remember persons, who set out in life together with us, but who have died—some of them, *we fear,* in their sins? It is melancholy to think of: but should we not melt with gratitude on our own account? They were cut off, and we are spared! Were we better than they? Rather let us confess, that we are altogether debtors to free grace, to rich and undeserved mercy!

But let us look on the bright side also. How many that have died before us, shone as examples of piety! Some were remarkable for the circumstances of their conversion; others, for the holy life they lived, glorifying Christ by abundant fruits of righteousness; while others left behind them a sweet recollection of their peaceful death, and many encouraging words to quicken us in our Christian course. Being dead, they yet speak to us. They animate our warmest hopes. They seem to say, "Follow us to glory!"

In a word, all that we have experienced, and all that we have seen, should lead to this conclusion—Let Man be humbled, and let our God and Saviour alone be exalted. Thrice blessed are they, whom the Lord teaches by his word, by his discipline, and by his Spirit! May you and I, my friend, be of that happy number!

PRAYER.

O Lord God Almighty, the refuge and strength of thy people in all generations: Hitherto thou hast been our Preserver and Guide; and thou requirest us to be mindful of all thy dealings with us, that we may learn to fear thee, to love thee, and to trust in thee, for our good always.

We would remember, O Lord, and acknowledge thy gracious hand, in the afflictions by which thou hast been pleased to chasten us: and we implore the quickening grace of thy Holy Spirit, to sanctify all our trials, that we may not suffer so many things in vain. If thou visit us with want or with losses, bestow on us a spirit of humble reliance on thy never-failing goodness, and thine all-sufficient grace. If disease and sickness be our lot, lead us to lament afresh our great unworthiness and vileness, and to seek special consolation and support from the pardoning love of our Saviour, and in the refreshing influences of thy Holy Spirit. Should death enter our dwellings, reminding us that this is not our rest, oh may our affections be loosened from the world, and surely fixed on things above! Where our treasure is, there may our heart be also.

We thank thee, O Lord, for that enlightening grace, whereby thou hast shown to us our own corruptions, and the mercy of Christ our Saviour to the chief of sinners. Thou hast humbled us, and proved us, that we might know what was in our heart. But oh, what depths of pride and self-will, of unbelief and ingratitude, have been discovered there! We must needs wonder at thy patience and thy long-suffering toward us. Truly the heart is deceitful above all things, and desperately wicked: who can know it? Thou, O Lord, searchest the heart; thou triest the reins. Thou knowest what we have been, and what we still are: our faults are not hid from thee. We entreat thee to forgive all our sins, and still be gracious unto us. Take away our dross, and purify our souls. And when thou hast prepared us by thine effectual grace, receive us at length into thy blessed presence, not for our worthiness, but for the alone merit of our compassionate High Priest and Saviour, Jesus Christ our Lord. Amen.

XXV.

THE CHARACTER OF JOSHUA.

JOSHUA i. 1—9.

Now after the death of Moses the servant of the Lord, it came to pass, that the Lord spake unto Joshua the son of Nun, Moses' minister, saying,

Moses my servant is dead; now therefore arise, go over this Jordan, thou, and all this people, unto the land which I do give to them, even to the children of Israel.

Every place that the sole of your foot shall tread upon, that have I given unto you, as I said unto Moses:

From the wilderness and this Lebanon even unto the great river, the river Euphrates, all the land of the Hittites, and unto the great sea toward the going down of the sun, shall be your coast.

There shall not any man be able to stand before thee all the days of thy life: as I was with Moses, so I will be with thee: I will not fail thee, nor forsake thee.

Be strong and of good courage: for unto this people shalt thou divide for an inheritance the land, which I sware unto their fathers to give them.

Only be thou strong and very courageous, that thou mayest observe to do according to all the law, which Moses my servant commanded thee: turn not from it to the right hand or to the left, that thou mayest prosper whithersoever thou goest.

This book of the law shall not depart out of thy mouth; but

thou shalt meditate therein day and night, that thou mayest observe to do according to all that is written therein: for then thou shalt make thy way prosperous, and then thou shalt have good success.

Have I not commanded thee? Be strong and of a good courage; be not afraid, neither be thou dismayed: for the Lord thy God is with thee, whithersoever thou goest.

A BRAVE man is everywhere an object of admiration. As we gaze at the hero who has endured hardships, faced dangers, fought battles and gained victories, we naturally are filled with wonder, reverence, and delight. Crowds flock to see the man: they follow him with shouts of applause: they feel as if they never could forget him.

But let us turn from these scenes of human pride, and meditate on a nobler subject—that of a religious warrior. The character of Joshua shines with a far brighter glory than what the world's heroes can boast;—a glory so exalted, that this servant of God was honoured by being made a Type of the Lord Jesus Christ.

What the Lord here enjoins, was fully complied with by Joshua. In fact, his whole history—before, as well as after this command—was one continued proof of his unshaken courage. Let us consider some instances of it.

1. First, it was no small honour, that he was appointed to command the Israelites in the first battle that they had to fight, after leaving Egypt. God had led them round, at first, by the way of the wilderness, that they might not see war. But at length, at Rephidim, the Amalekites came and

opposed them. On this occasion, "Moses said unto Joshua, Choose us out men, and go out, fight with Amalek: to-morrow I will stand on the top of the hill with the rod of God in mine hand. So Joshua did as Moses had said to him, and fought with Amalek: and Moses, Aaron, and Hur, went up to the top of the hill. And it came to pass, when Moses held up his hand, that Israel prevailed: and when he let down his hand, Amalek prevailed. But Moses' hands were heavy; and they took a stone, and put it under him, and he sat thereon; and Aaron and Hur stayed up his hands, the one on the one side, and the other on the other side; and his hands were steady until the going down of the sun. And Joshua discomfited Amalek and his people with the edge of the sword."

You will say, perhaps, that this was soldierly courage. It was so: but it was much more;—it was the courage of Faith, animated by Prayer. Moses had concerted with Joshua, that the one should pray, whilst the other was to fight. You will observe, therefore, that each of these holy men shared, though in different ways, in the battle. Moses exerted every nerve in prayer: while Joshua was at one and the same instant attacking Amalek, and lifting up his heart, together with Moses, Aaron and Hur, and all believing Israelites, to the throne of grace.—The glory of the victory was ascribed, as was most due, to the favour of the Almighty. After the battle, Moses built an altar, and named it Jehovah-Nissi; which signifies, The Lord is my banner.

2. Joshua sustained, also, the office of Moses' minister, or servant; and attended him on Mount Sinai, remaining there forty days, alone, while Moses went to the top of the mount. Humble courage must have filled the heart of Joshua, during the whole of this solemn season. How different from the wanton, fickle, impatient temper of the Israelites at the foot of the mountain; who gave up Moses for lost, and set up the golden calf, and worshipped it!

3. It was a very signal instance of the courage of Joshua, that he, together with Caleb, gave a good account of the land of Canaan, at the time when the other ten spies spread a disheartening report, saying, "We be not able to go up against the people; for they are stronger than we:" "we were in our own sight as grasshoppers, and so we were in their sight." Base and cowardly spirit! And so feeble-minded were the Israelites, that they fell into the same unbelieving temper, and were ready to stone Joshua and Caleb, for telling them that the land was an exceeding good land;—for saying, "Let us go up at once and possess it; for we are well able to overcome it."

4. Hence followed a necessity for exerting an entirely different kind of courage. Joshua had now to bear, in his proportion, the almost insufferable manners of the people in the wilderness for forty years. He had to exercise Patience. There is much of true courage in patience. To bear the repeated provocations of unreasonable and wicked

men, is a most severe trial of temper. The spirit of Moses, you will remember, did not hold out: his patience and meekness forsook him, so that he spake unadvisedly with his lips: for which sin he was excluded from Canaan.

5. The courage of Joshua was, no doubt, greatly increased by the animating language addressed to him, at the time of his succeeding to Moses. Who can read those expressions, " Be strong; be of a good courage; the Lord thy God is with thee," without feeling that the heart of Joshua must have been raised to the highest pitch of holy confidence in God? His courage was founded on the command and word of God. Read again that remarkable verse, " This book of the law shall not depart out of thy mouth; but thou shalt meditate therein day and night, that thou mayest observe to do according to all that is written therein: for then thou shalt make thy way prosperous, and then thou shalt have good success." Here was the secret of his bravery: he was true to his God; and God was faithful in performing his gracious promises to his servant.

6. Even in his old age, not long before his death, Joshua addressed his countrymen in words which showed his steady devotedness to his God: " As for me and my house, we will serve the Lord." Here we see him bold, both as a public character, and also in private and domestic life. There has been many a warrior, not afraid to face an army in the field, who has nevertheless feared to stand out

against a scoffing, irreligious world — has feared even to assemble together his own household and dependants, to worship God!

Having considered the exemplary Courage of Joshua, let me now set him before you as an eminent Type of Christ.

1. His very name shows resemblance; Joshua and Jesus both signifying, a Saviour.

2. In his commanding the people of God, Joshua was a type of Christ. For Jesus bears the government on his shoulder. " All power is given unto him in heaven and in earth," for the good of his Church. He is the " Captain of our salvation."

3. In conquering the enemies of the people of God, they are both alike. " Jesus shall reign, till he hath put all enemies under his feet."

4. Joshua brought the people out of the wilderness, into Canaan; and gave to them their portions of land by lot. Jesus, with zeal, wisdom, and love incomparably greater, delivers us from this present evil world;—he hath purchased for us an heavenly inheritance;— and he assures his beloved followers, that he will bring them into the possession of that inheritance: " In my Father's house are many mansions....... I go to prepare a place for you. And if I go and prepare a place for you, I will come again, and receive you unto myself; that where I am, there ye may be also."

My friend, how delightful is it, when reading the Old Testament, to observe that it constantly points to the New! How delightful, everywhere in the

Bible to discover Christ! Let us then be encouraged to become his devoted followers! Let us put on the whole armour of God: let us wage war against sin, the world, and the devil: let us press forward, with Jesus as our Leader, still conquering and to conquer. And oh may we attain, finally, to that rest, which "remaineth for the people of God!"

PRAYER.

O Lord Jesu Christ, who by thine almighty power hast overcome death, and opened unto us the gate of everlasting life: Give us grace boldly to follow thee, and manfully to fight, under thy banner, against sin, the world, and the devil; and to continue thy faithful soldiers and servants, unto our life's end. To whom else should we go, or what other lord should we obey? Thou hast the words of eternal life; and thou hast redeemed us unto God by thy blood. Oh that we may renounce and forsake all other masters, and cleave unto thee with full purpose of heart! May we have no fellowship with the unfruitful works of darkness, and never halt between two opinions. Suffer us not to yield: strengthen us to fight the good fight of faith, and to lay hold on eternal life.

Lord, we confess with shame, that, through the frailty of our nature and the weakness of our faith, we do not always withstand the enemies of our souls. Pardon our want of holy zeal, and all our manifold sins and infirmities. Hear the prayers and intercessions which are offered up by the whole Church of God on earth, that not one of thy people may faint or fall. Support those that are feeble and downcast in spirit, and let thy strength be perfected in their weakness. Grant to all thy servants such an assurance of thy presence with them, and of thy word commanding them, that they may never be dismayed, and never turn back. By the power of the Holy Ghost, cause us daily to wax stronger and stronger in spirit. Enable us, O Lord, to overcome every hindrance: deliver us out of all temptations, and give us victory over sin and Satan. Crown us at length with the crown of glory, that fadeth not away: and to Thee, O Jesus, the Strength of our life, and the Captain of our salvation, will we ascribe all honour and power and dominion, now and for ever. Amen.

XXVI.

THE CITIES OF REFUGE.

Joshua xx. 1—6.

The Lord spake unto Joshua, saying,

Speak to the children of Israel, saying, Appoint out for you cities of refuge, whereof I spake unto you by the hand of Moses:

That the slayer that killeth any person unawares and unwittingly may flee thither: and they shall be your refuge from the avenger of blood.

And when he that doth flee unto one of those cities shall stand at the entering of the gate of the city, and shall declare his cause in the ears of the elders of that city, they shall take him into the city unto them, and give him a place, that he may dwell among them

And if the avenger of blood pursue after him, then they shall not deliver the slayer up into his hand; because he smote his neighbour unwittingly, and hated him not beforetime.

And he shall dwell in that city, until he stand before the congregation for judgment, and until the death of the high-priest that shall be in those days: then shall the slayer return, and come unto his own city, and unto his own house, unto the city from whence he fled.

The life of man is so precious in the sight of our Creator, that he has denounced the heaviest judgments upon the crime of murder. He has also implanted in our breasts a natural horror and detestation of it. Even the accidental killing of a fellow-creature was, by the Jewish customs, liable to be punished by the next of kin; who was thence called "the avenger of blood." In order to help innocent persons in escaping that vengeance, it pleased God to appoint, at convenient distances in the land, six cities of refuge; and to enjoin, that the man-slayer, who had killed any person at unawares, and hated him not aforetime, should flee thither and be protected.

In this humane law we behold a remarkable emblem of Man's Salvation by Christ. Let us consider the various circumstances of the man-slayer, and show how the case of every sinner resembles his. And may the Spirit of God so fill us with alarm on account of our dangerous condition, that we may be constrained to flee unto Jesus, as our only refuge from the wrath to come!

1. We must first remark, that there is one point in which we, as sinners, differ wholly from the man-

slayer. His case was that of a man killing a fellow-creature purely by accident: our case is that of sinners who have ten thousand times sinned *wilfully*, in thought, word, and deed. It is true, some of our sins have been what are called sins of ignorance: but, was not our ignorance itself sinful? Why were we ignorant of God's law? Were we not wilfully ignorant? Truly we need pardon for our sins of negligence, as well as for those which have been manifestly wilful and presumptuous.

2. The city of Refuge offered its protection to the manslayer. Other cities, however safe in other respects, yet gave him no security. So, for us sinners, there is One Saviour given: He is the only refuge for our guilty souls. We are not to choose our own way of salvation, but to take that which God has mercifully provided for us. One man may talk thus, "I will try to earn salvation, by becoming good:"—another, "I will say many prayers, give much alms, and set a far better example than I have done hitherto." Now, these things in themselves are good: it is right for us to amend our doings. But this is not *the appointed way of salvation*. We cannot by *our own works purchase* forgiveness: we cannot thus escape wrath. Jesus saith, "I am the way, and the truth, and the life: no man cometh unto the Father, but by me." "Neither is there salvation in any other: for there is none other name under heaven given among men, whereby we must be saved."

3. The manslayer who knew this law, would

naturally, as soon as he saw his danger, think of the city of Refuge as his security. Just the same is the case of a sinner, when alarmed by the discovery of his perishing state, and made acquainted with the Gospel. His heart turns to Christ. Faith in Christ is the only thing now for him. Faith, owning Christ as able and willing to save from death, is the proper spirit of mind for an awakened sinner. Not only must we despair of every other help; but we must be assured and convinced in our hearts, that Christ is a sufficient Helper and Redeemer. Believing in Christ, is fleeing to the city of Refuge.

If now you should imagine that a mere general notion of believing in Christ is sufficient for salvation, let me guard you against so dangerous an error. Consider carefully, what kind of faith alone is genuine and scriptural. For example, inquire— Do you come to Jesus, really grieving for sin, and resolving, through the help of his Spirit, to go and sin no more? Do you determine to glorify God in your body and in your spirit, which are God's? Do you unreservedly give up yourself to him? Is your faith, simple; your love, pure; your obedience, unfeigned?—This strict self-examination is needed, to prevent the gross presumption of supposing that we can be safe in Christ, whilst yet willingly remaining in sin.

4. Observe further, that when the man-slayer was once securely lodged in the city of Refuge, he was safe for life. But then it was on condition of

his continuing within the walls of the city, and never going out till the death of the high-priest, during whose priesthood he had fled to the city. So, when we have come to Christ for salvation, we must "abide in him." Daily pardon, daily renewal unto holiness, daily communion with him by prayer—this is what is meant by our abiding in him. The life which we now live, we must live by faith in the Son of God, who loved us, and gave himself for us. Thus are we placed, and thus are we kept, out of danger: we are safe, for Time and for Eternity. We are "saved with an everlasting salvation."

5. It is related by ancient writers, that the Jews were accustomed to keep the roads leading to these cities in good repair; and that where any doubt might arise, from two or three roads meeting, a sign was put up, with the word REFUGE written on it in large letters, to show which was the way to the city. Thus should we, by every possible means, make it plain to our perishing fellow-sinners, which is the true, the sure, the only way of salvation. The road should be cleared of all false doctrines, which might mislead the trembling penitent, or stumble a weak believer. And what else should we set before your eyes, but words such as these— Look unto Jesus!—Take this path, the good old path of the Bible; and you will escape from the wrath to come. "Believe in the Lord Jesus Christ, and thou shalt be saved."

6. In these cities there would probably be several

persons dwelling at the same time, indebted to this law of mercy. We may easily conceive how they would converse together about their peculiar privilege; and, likewise, how eagerly they would welcome each new-comer, who might be under the necessity of taking refuge like themselves. Should they see any one closely followed by the avenger of blood, and but just able to escape, how would they throw open the gates of the city, and pull him in! All this may teach us how happy we should be to speak to one another concerning the blessings of salvation; and how earnestly we ought to labour in inviting others to " win Christ, and be found in Him."

In a word, my friend, let us think of ourselves, as of persons in danger of death, even of eternal death.—The avenger of blood is upon thee! Satan, the enemy, the accuser, the destroyer of souls, demands at God's hands that thou shouldest be consigned to endless torments, for thy sins. The law of God condemns thee, and thine own conscience must plead guilty.—What wilt thou do? Whither wilt thou flee?—Behold, Jesus is near! Like a man hastening to the cities of refuge—cities so conveniently situated that one of them might easily be reached in half a day—so mayest thou, at any hour, run with a believing heart to Jesus; and he is immediately at hand to deliver.

But fly speedily: for, what if Death and Judgment should overtake thee, before thy repentance—before thou hast found salvation in Christ! Delay not an hour—not a moment! Give neither sleep to thine eyes, nor slumber to thine eyelids, till thou hast gained pardon, peace, and the gift of a new heart, through faith in Christ Jesus!

PRAYER.

O Lord, who hast graciously revealed to us the way of pardon and acceptance with thee, through faith in Christ Jesus: Hasten us, that we delay not to come unto Him for the life and salvation of our souls. Our sins have deserved thy wrath: and we might justly fear lest thine indignation should burn against us like a consuming fire. But we bow before thee, pleading the merits of Jesus, the Lamb of God, who was slain to take away the sins of the world. For his sake we beseech thee to forgive us all our sins, negligences, and ignorances. Save us from eternal death: translate us into the kingdom of thy dear Son: and grant that we may henceforth walk as the children of thy grace, and heirs of eternal life.

Have compassion, O Lord, on the multitudes of careless sinners, who walk on still in darkness, and know not that the wrath of God abideth on them. Awaken them, ere it be too late: lead them to mourn with a godly sorrow for their sins, and to flee from the wrath to come. May they look unto Jesus, and be saved through faith in Him.

Grant, Lord, to those who have fled to Christ as their Refuge, that they may have grace to continue in his love. Oh, suffer us not, through unbelief and carelessness, to fall away from Him. Bestow on us the anointing of thy Holy Spirit, to comfort, guide, and stablish us. Cause us to abide in Christ; that when He shall appear, we may have confidence, and not be ashamed before him at his coming.

We ask these mercies for the sake of the same Jesus Christ, our only Lord and Saviour. Amen.

XXVII.
SAMUEL, A PATTERN TO THE YOUNG.
1 Samuel iii. 1—10.

And the child Samuel ministered unto the Lord before Eli. And the word of the Lord was precious in those days; there was no open vision.

And it came to pass at this time, when Eli was laid down in his place, and his eyes began to wax dim, that he could not see;

And ere the lamp of God went out in the temple of the Lord, where the ark of God was, and Samuel was laid down to sleep;

That the Lord called Samuel: and he answered, Here am I.

And he ran unto Eli, and said, Here am I; for thou calledst me. And he said, I called not; lie down again. And he went and lay down.

And the Lord called yet again, Samuel. And Samuel arose and went to Eli, and said, Here am I; for thou didst call me. And he answered, I called not, my son; lie down again.

Now Samuel did not yet know the Lord, neither was the word of the Lord yet revealed unto him.

And the Lord called Samuel again the third time. And he arose and went to Eli, and said, Here am I; for thou didst call me. And Eli perceived that the Lord had called the child.

Therefore Eli said unto Samuel, Go, lie down: and it shall be, if he call thee, that thou shalt say, Speak, Lord; for thy servant heareth. So Samuel went and lay down in his place.

And the Lord came, and stood, and called as at other times, Samuel, Samuel. Then Samuel answered, Speak; for thy servant heareth.

THE character of Samuel is a pattern to us all; and especially to the young. When we find a person so eminent for piety as he was, it is natural to ask how he began his course in life.

The circumstances of his childhood were remarkably favourable to his growth in piety. Both his parents were pious: his mother's devout spirit is particularly mentioned. From his tenderest age, she dedicated him to the Lord; and God mercifully answered her prayers, so that Samuel became the Lord's servant, and continued such, all the days of his life.

Observe, then, Samuel's conduct, when he entered upon life. He was appointed to minister unto the Lord before Eli. This was a dangerous situation; for the sons of Eli were the worst possible example that he could have. Eli himself was growing blind, and had never been sufficiently strict with his family. In such a situation, if Samuel had been a graceless youth, he would have thought only of pleasing himself; and would have accounted it a tedious task, to wait on this old man, trimming the lamps, and opening and shutting the doors of the House of the Lord. But on the contrary, every thing shows him to have been dutiful and devout. It is said, that "the child Samuel grew on, and was in favour both with the Lord and also with men." No doubt he avoided, as much as possible, those wicked men, the sons of Eli. Like David (whom he afterwards anointed to be king over Israel), Samuel could say, "I had rather be a door-keeper in the House of my God, than to dwell in the tents of wickedness."

Eli was, we hope, a good man; but he was grievously negligent of his duty to his sons, whom he ought to have punished severely. As *they* were so undutiful and ungodly, he seems to have adopted Samuel; whom he affectionately calls, "My son." It is somewhat mournful to receive more kindness from others, than from our own kindred.

At length the Lord revealed himself to Samuel: this was while Samuel was yet a child. There were in those days no prophets; or, as it is expressed, "There was no open vision:" so that the people of Israel knew not whither to go, to inquire the will of the Lord. God, however, was now intending to establish Samuel as his prophet—the child being at this time about twelve years of age. It is said, He did not yet know the Lord; that is, he had not before this received any special revelation from heaven: consequently, he did not know the way in which God would manifest himself. When, therefore, the Lord called him by name, in the night-season, he thought it was the voice of Eli, and repeatedly rose to go to him. Eli at length perceived that it was the Lord who called him; and directed him therefore, when next called, to answer, "Speak, Lord; for thy servant heareth."

The words are few and simple; yet they signify much:—"Speak, Lord; for thy servant heareth." Let me endeavour, by means of them, to fix two reflections upon your heart.

1. First of all, in saying, " Speak, Lord"— Samuel expressed his *Desire to know* God's will. He was all attention. " Thy servant heareth." This may admonish us, who enjoy greater religious privileges than Samuel did, to pray devoutly, and read the word of God diligently, that we may know his will. To us God speaks in the Bible: from that blessed book we may learn, who God is, and what we ourselves are. There, too, we may learn the way of salvation; how perishing sinners are redeemed from hell, and reconciled to God by the death of Christ Jesus. Salvation is " the one thing needful;" and if we are awake, as young Samuel was, we shall seek for it in our Bibles, with as much seriousness as if we heard God speaking to us with his voice. We shall pray likewise for the teaching of the Holy Spirit; according to those words of David, " Open thou mine eyes, that I may behold wondrous things out of thy law."

2. But further, Samuel's words express also his *Readiness to obey* the will of the Lord. His heart and life were given to God: therefore he uses the words, " Thy servant." He could with truth say, " I am thy servant; I have chosen thy service, and I love it. I have loved the habitation of thy House, and the place where thine honour dwelleth." When he says, " Thy servant heareth," he means, Thy servant is ready to obey.

Consider, then, the following plain and weighty questions:—Have *you* this devout and praying heart; this understanding heart; this obedient heart? Have you been taught to discern between good and evil? Do you refuse the evil, and choose the good? Have you discovered how corrupt and sinful you are; and have you sought pardon through Christ? Have you felt the natural evil of your heart; and implored the gift of the Holy Spirit, to take away the heart of stone, and give you a heart of flesh? Do you love prayer? Do you value your Bible; and do you love the House of God? Are you shocked at evil company, and do you shun it? Do you value the friendship of the godly?

These are questions which we may profitably ask ourselves, when studying the character of young Samuel. Oh may you be led, like him, to love, serve, and obey your Heavenly Father; to walk before the Lord unto all well pleasing; and to enjoy the light of his countenance, while he smiles upon you as upon one of his adopted children!

PRAYER.

O Lord, who hast in great mercy given unto us thy holy word, that from it we may learn thy will, and be guided into the way of life everlasting: We thank thee for this precious light;—a light which many prophets and righteous men have desired to see, and have not seen it. O grant us also the gift of thy quickening and enlightening Spirit, that we may in truth be taught of God. Let faith be mixed with what we read and hear from thy word. Dispose us to embrace its promises with holy joy, and to order our conversation by its blessed precepts.

Implant in our hearts the spirit of affectionate and obedient children. Draw us, and we will run after thee; yea, our delight shall be in thy commandments.

We beseech thee to look graciously upon all young persons, and to deliver them from the many snares which beset them on every side. Dispose them to take good heed to their paths, and in all things to make their choice according to thy word. Let the knowledge of thy Holy Scriptures lead them to faith in Christ Jesus, that they may obtain eternal salvation through him. Cause them to grow up as plants in their youth, and hereafter may they bring forth fruit in their age, to the glory of thy name, and the good of mankind: and receive them and us, finally, to thine eternal Kingdom, through Jesus Christ our Lord. Amen.

XXVIII.

DAVID'S SIN AND PARDON.

2 SAMUEL xii. 1—14.

And the Lord sent Nathan unto David. And he came unto him, and said unto him, There were two men in one city; the one rich, and the other poor.

The rich man had exceeding many flocks and herds:

But the poor man had nothing, save one little ewe-lamb, which he had bought and nourished up: and it grew up together with him, and with his children; it did eat of his own meat, and drank of his own cup, and lay in his bosom, and was unto him as a daughter.

And there came a traveller unto the rich man, and he spared

to take of his own flock and of his own herd, to dress for the wayfaring man that was come unto him; but took the poor man's lamb, and dressed it for the man that was come to him.

And David's anger was greatly kindled against the man; and he said to Nathan, As the Lord liveth, the man that hath done this thing shall surely die:

And he shall restore the lamb fourfold, because he did this thing, and because he had no pity.

And Nathan said to David, Thou art the man. Thus saith the Lord God of Israel, I anointed thee king over Israel, and I delivered thee out of the hand of Saul;

And I gave thee thy master's house, and thy master's wives into thy bosom, and gave thee the house of Israel and of Judah; and if that had been too little, I would moreover have given unto thee such and such things.

Wherefore hast thou despised the commandment of the Lord, to do evil in his sight? Thou hast killed Uriah the Hittite with the sword, and hast taken his wife to be thy wife, and hast slain him with the sword of the children of Ammon.

Now therefore the sword shall never depart from thine house; because thou hast despised me, and hast taken the wife of Uriah the Hittite to be thy wife.

Thus saith the Lord, Behold, I will raise up evil against thee out of thine own house; and I will take thy wives from before thine eyes, and give them unto thy neighbour, and he shall lie with thy wives in the sight of this sun.

For thou didst it secretly: but I will do this thing before all Israel, and before the sun.

And David said unto Nathan, I have sinned against the Lord. And Nathan said unto David, The Lord also hath put away thy sin; thou shalt not die.

Howbeit, because by this deed thou hast given great occasion to the enemies of the Lord to blaspheme, the child also that is born unto thee shall surely die.

IT has pleased God, in the Holy Scriptures, to describe his Saints, not as models of perfection, but as they really were; namely, as frail and sinful creatures, saved only through grace. One Person —and one only—is presented to us as perfect, the Lord Jesus Christ: while concerning others, we know that they are all alike—full of evil. Whatever holiness any may possess, springs only from their being born anew of the Holy Spirit: and even they are to be as our patterns, only so far as they are made like unto Christ, by divine grace.

Thus was David made, by the Holy Spirit, "a man after God's own heart." But by his falling into sin, he showed that a great degree of corruption still remained in him. Ignorant men are stumbled at his character: they think it impossible that one who sinned so grossly could ever have been a pious man. But humble men are comforted, to see that one, fallen so deeply, could yet be raised up again, and restored to God's favour, and to holiness.

May the Holy Spirit make this part of David's history profitable to our souls! Let us observe— How deep was his repentance; and how gracious his recovery.

1. In order to bring David to repentance, Nathan, the prophet, was sent to him by the Lord. He came with a pointed message, delivered in the form of a parable. It was directly aimed at David's case: yet it was so skilfully put, that David did not see the drift of it; but took it simply as an account of the cruelty of one of his subjects. Having heard the case, he proceeded to pass sentence of death on the person guilty. In so doing he, in fact, con-

demned himself. Nathan immediately addressed the king in plain words, saying, "Thou art the man." David, whose conscience probably had often before been uneasy, instantly felt the sting of Nathan's rebuke, and confessed—"I have sinned against the Lord!"

Observe how closely Nathan fastens conviction on his mind.—He shows him the *source* of his sin! he had "despised the Lord." David had felt no concern for the dishonour he was bringing on Religion: or, if conscience had in some degree checked him, yet he had slighted the check. Conscience is God's deputy: he, therefore, who resists his own conscience, despises God.—Again, Nathan reminds him of the *aggravations* of his guilt. How many mercies had David received, which should have bound him to God's service! How much light had shone on his path! What abundant grace had been vouchsafed to the sweet Psalmist of Israel; so that greater holiness was to be expected of him than of other men! Yet all this was sacrificed to gratify a base lust.—Then Nathan points out the dreadful *amount* of guilt:—Bathsheba dishonoured; Uriah and others murdered; Joab used as the tool and partner of these murders; the enemies of the Lord at home, and the Ammonites abroad, encouraged to triumph and blaspheme! In short, David had multiplied immensely the sins and miseries of other persons, as well as his own. —All these things were brought home to his conscience, by the faithful prophet of the Lord.

2. Now, if David had been a proud, hard, impenitent man, he would have fired at this reproof of Nathan. He would probably have banished him from court; or even have felt inclined to put him to death. Saul would have done so. But David was a child of God : grace touched him : grace recovered him. See how he bends beneath the rebuke. He cannot deny the charge: he attempts no defence: he makes no excuses. He answers from the bottom of his heart—" I have sinned against the Lord !"

Perhaps you may think it was an easy matter for him to make this confession: the words are so few, and his guilt was so clear. Ah, my friend ! you forget, surely, how long David's heart had been hardening in sullen silence. The fewness of his words arose from the overwhelming anguish of his soul. He abhorred himself. He felt himself to be vile in God's sight. Meditate on these marks of godly sorrow; and you will see, that although David's words were very few, yet they expressed every thing. " I "—I am indeed that guilty wretch whom I have myself just condemned: yea, I am viler far than he. " I have sinned;'—no longer can I hide my crime, or smother the confession of it. " Against the Lord;"—he is the Being most dishonoured, most offended. True, I have sinned fearfully against Bathsheba, Uriah, Joab, and many others; yea, against the whole Church of God: but my sin *against the Lord* is so enormous, that it comprehends and surpasses all the rest. " Against thee, thee only, have I sinned, and done this evil in thy sight."

Full confession opens a ready way for the message of free pardon. Nathan is commissioned immediately to declare to David, "The Lord also hath put away thy sin." When genuine repentance begins, forgiveness is near at hand. "If we confess our sins"—that is, hating and forsaking them—then, "God is faithful and just to forgive us our sins, and to cleanse us from all unrighteousness."

Comfortable words, "The Lord also hath put away thy sin!" But, oh! where does the Lord lay that load of guilt?—On Christ! The curse of all our sins falls on His head! "All we like sheep have gone astray: we have turned every one to his own way: and the Lord hath laid on Him the iniquity of us all."

Wonderful love and pity of our Redeemer; that he should come to seek and to save that which was lost—to set free the slaves of Satan—to recover those who, like David, had once broken the snare of the devil, but had been again entangled and therein overcome! Surely we must exclaim, "Where sin abounded, there did grace much more abound!"

The soul of David is now kept from sinking in despair. He receives both pardoning and refreshing grace.—But does he continue in sin, that grace may abound? Oh, no! he returns to the service of the Lord with humble prayer. It was on this occasion that he wrote his penitential Psalm—the

Fifty-first: which whosoever reads, must see that he was restored to the love of holiness.

But lest David himself, or any others, should forget that sin is vile and dangerous, God appointed many outward punishments soon to fall heavily on David and his house. The Lord is a God jealous for the honour of his name. Witness the scene of David's dying child—the rebellion and untimely death of his son Absalom—his many family-troubles, and the sore judgments that fell upon his kingdom. All these calamities were intended to show what an evil and bitter thing it is, to depart from the living God. The Lord restores his servants; but it is by the way of deep humiliation. He does not suffer them to shake off their feelings of shame and grief. Let us draw near to him, brokenhearted: and while pardon is pronounced, let us rejoice with trembling.

PRAYER.

Have mercy upon us, O God, according to thy loving-kindness: according unto the multitude of thy tender mercies, blot out our transgressions. Wash us thoroughly from our iniquity, and cleanse us from our sin. For we acknowledge our transgressions, and our sin is ever before us.

Lord, we are not able to number all the offences by which we have transgressed against thee, in thought, word, and deed. Many of them were committed before we knew thy holy law, while we were yet living in ignorance of Thee. And if thy mercy now hath brought us to delight in thy service, still we are encompassed with infirmities, and in many things we sin continually. Hide thy face from our sins, O Lord, and blot out all our iniquities. Cleanse our souls in the fountain of the Redeemer's blood. Though our sins be as scarlet, let them be as white as snow: though they be red like crimson, let them be as wool.

Lord, we confess before thee the corruption and vileness of our nature. Sin hath polluted our imagination, our affections, and our memory. Our mind is darkened and our conscience defiled; yea, the very spring of our thoughts is unclean. We were shapen in iniquity: we were born in sin: we are by nature children of wrath. There is no difference between us and the worst of men, but what thy free grace hath wrought: and, oh! what cause have we to blush and be confounded, at the remembrance that we have so little improved the light and knowledge which we enjoy. Alas! how far short do we fall of our high calling in Christ Jesus!

Lord, create in us a clean heart, and renew a right spirit within us. Cast us not away from thy presence: take not thy Holy Spirit from us. Uphold us with thy free Spirit. Enable us to rejoice in thee, and live to thy glory, accounting thy service perfect freedom.

Forgive us, O Lord, those iniquities more especially, by which we have caused others to sin. We would lay our hand upon our mouth, when we reflect how we have even tempted others to commit iniquity: and too often, alas! we have been a stumbling-block and an offence to thine own children. Deliver us from this burden of guilt, O God, thou God of our salvation. Open our lips, that we may with earnestness and affection extol thy pardoning mercy, and thy renewing grace. Give us wisdom to lead many wandering souls to Christ; especially from among those with whom we once joined in folly and sin.

O Thou that despisest not the sighing of a contrite heart, nor the desire of such as be sorrowful; let thy merciful ears be open unto our prayer. Accept, and bless us: and do for us even more than we have asked, through the riches of thy grace in Christ our Lord. Amen.

XXIX.

DEATH OF AN INFANT.

2 Samuel xii. 18—23.

And it came to pass on the seventh day, that the child died. And the servants of David feared to tell him that the child was dead; for they said, Behold, while the child was yet alive, we spake unto him, and he would not hearken unto our voice: how will he then vex himself, if we tell him that the child is dead?

But when David saw that the servants whispered, David perceived that the child was dead: therefore David said unto his servants, Is the child dead? And they said, He is dead.

Then David arose from the earth, and washed and anointed himself, and changed his apparel, and came into the house of the Lord, and worshipped: then he came to his own house; and when he required, they set bread before him, and he did eat.

Then said his servants unto him, What thing is this that thou last done? thou didst fast and weep for the child, while it was alive; but when the child was dead, thou didst rise and eat bread.

And he said, While the child was yet alive, I fasted and wept: for I said, Who can tell whether God will be gracious to me, that the child may live?

But now he is dead, wherefore should I fast? can I bring him back again? I shall go to him, but he shall not return to me.

THE manner in which different persons behave under affliction, is exceedingly various. Some cry aloud: others mourn in silence. Some have their burst of grief beforehand; others—which is perhaps more common—after the bereavement. There is no uniformity in these matters: but it is the bounden duty of the servants of God, while suffering natural tears to have their flow, yet at the same time to turn to the Lord who smites them, and meekly to kiss the rod.

David had a bitter cup to drink of, in the sickness and death of his little child. Let us learn from him some useful lessons, which may be seasonable to us when in similar afflictions.

1. It would be painful to David to see the poor little infant suffering, and the mother watching over it with tender anxiety; yet, as he had reason to fear, with no hope of its recovery. It pierces the heart of father and mother to hear the moans of a helpless babe, and to feel how little can be done to relieve it. It struggles on awhile, and cries, and pants, and is convulsed, till at length it breathes its last breath, and becomes a pale corpse. And all this, for what? Not for sins actually committed by that infant; but because it inherits the curse lying

on Adam and all his race. God hereby proves to us, that sin has tainted and ruined all the family of mankind; and he marks in the clearest manner his abhorrence of sin. Here we see death reigning over one that has "not sinned after the similitude of Adam's transgression"—that is, not wilfully or knowingly: yet, as being his offspring, it is involved in that wide-sweeping sentence, "In the day that thou eatest thereof, thou shalt surely die." "In Adam all die." "By one man sin entered into the world, and death by sin."—Who can dispute the righteous judgment of God? or who can resist His will? Let us bow, and adore!

2. The merciful provisions of the Covenant of grace, should, at such a time, be fully set before our view. In David's mind there was good hope, that, through the infinite merits of the Redeemer, this poor infant rested with God. He doubted not, but that its soul was now for ever set free from the curse, and that its short season of anguish was exchanged for a glorious and immortal life, through Jesus Christ.

3. Yet there were some peculiarly humbling thoughts which could not fail to rush into David's mind, and keep him very low in his own eyes. This child was the fruit of sin; and its death was designed as a signal mark of God's displeasure against that sin. In this way alone could the mouth of blasphemers, the enemies of the Lord, be stopped: (2 Samuel xii. 14.)

When we are called to suffer deep affliction of

any kind, it may not always be possible to trace a connection between our sin and its punishment. Thus much, however, is certain:—if there had been no sin, there would have been no suffering in the world: and therefore affliction should always lead us to renewed exercises of sorrow for sin.

4. The case of David may teach us how we ought to behave *beforehand*, ere the affliction comes; and especially at a time when the rod appears to be closely hanging over us. Humble prayer should then be our work and our comfort. In the case of this infant, while mother, nurse, and physician were all doing their best to save life, David made it his special office to intercede for the poor little-one. He fasted, he wept, he lay upon the earth; he withdrew from ordinary society, that he might give himself unto prayer. He prayed, hoping against hope. He prayed as one that knew the power of Prayer; for prayer has often stayed the hand of wrath, and moved the tenderest compassions of the Lord our God. "Like as a father pitieth his children, so the Lord pitieth them that fear him."

5. The example of David shows us also how we should conduct ourselves *after* afflictions.

There seems to have been a holy cheerfulness imparted immediately to the soul of David, as soon as he heard that the worst was over. The Spirit of consolation lifted him up from the earth; carried him to the House of God; bent his knees in adoration; and strengthened him to spread forth his hands in praise. The same free Spirit led him back to his household and family, and there enabled him to speak a few words, full of Resignation and Hope: " Now the child is dead, wherefore should I fast? Can I bring him back again? I shall go to him, but he shall not return to me."

What a comfort, that God hath not only permitted us to weep, but hath likewise appointed " a time to refrain from weeping." Yet some there are who refuse to be comforted: they seem to be in love with grief, and act as if they "did well to be angry." For what else is it, but rebellion against the Most High, to cherish sorrow long after the affliction is past? Was not the Lord wise and just, kind and good, in sending the rod of chastisement? May not indulged sorrow grow into a kind of sullen resentment against God? Does it not tend to prevent peaceful, sweet communion with him? And is it not sure to keep us back from many active duties, which demand our attention?

Reason itself teaches, that grief cannot bring back the beloved object, whose loss we so bitterly deplore. But the Gospel does far more for us. It reveals to us that exceeding and eternal weight of glory, which is prepared for all who die in the Lord. When, therefore, a little infant sleeps in Jesus; or when a departed relative or friend has left good evidence that he was the Lord's, we should aim at following him to glory: saying with affectionate desire, " I shall go to him!" And having this hope, we should, as it were, arise and shake ourselves from the dust, and put on our beautiful garments; once more take our harp from off the willows, and sing joyfully, " O give thanks unto the Lord, for he is good ;—for his mercy endureth for ever."

PRAYER.

Righteous art thou, O Lord, in thy judgments, and in all thy dealings with the children of men. None can stay thine hand, or say unto thee, What doest thou? We adore thee for thine infinite holiness; and we humbly acknowledge thy justice in the punishment of sin. Thou art of purer eyes than to behold iniquity, and wilt by no means clear the guilty. We confess that we have grievously offended against thee, and have deserved thy displeasure: but, O Heavenly Father, be not angry with us for ever: in wrath remember mercy. For thy dear Son's sake, pardon all our transgressions. Blot them out of the book of thy remembrance. Deal not with us after our sins, neither reward us according to our iniquities.

Lord, when thou layest thy chastening hand upon our families, and takest away any that are dear to us, enable us meekly to bow to thy holy will, and to believe that thou doest all things well. The Lord gave, and the Lord hath taken away: blessed be the name of the Lord !

Sanctify to us, O Lord, all our remaining family-comforts. We know not how soon they may be taken away from us, or we removed from them. Cause us to pass the time of our sojourning here in fear: and let thy Name be glorified by us, in all that we do, and in all that we suffer. Let us not yield to a spirit of complaining, or of unbelief. Shed abroad in our hearts the abundant consolations of thy Spirit. Though thou hast caused grief, yet have compassion upon us, according to the multitude of thy mercies. Make us glad according to the days wherein thou hast afflicted us, and the years wherein we have seen evil. Return, O Lord of Hosts; show the light of thy countenance, and we shall be whole.

Hear us, for the sake of Jesus Christ, our Mediator and Advocate. Amen.

XXX.

DANGEROUS SICKNESS OF A YOUNG PERSON.

2 SAMUEL xii. 22.

Who can tell whether God will be gracious unto me?

THE affecting history of David's conduct on occasion of the sickness and death of his infant child, may lead our minds yet further, in a channel of profitable reflection. Let us turn from the particular case of David; and inquire, with calm but solemn interest—What ought to be our feelings and conduct, when expecting to lose some beloved relative of maturer age?

It may be a son or a daughter, grown up to years of discretion, who is lying on the bed of languishing. What shall the anxious parent think and do now? In other words, What shall he say to his own heart—to the God of all grace—and to the Sufferer, whose last hour is gradually approaching? —I will endeavour to tell you.

1. It is a time when a pious parent may well ask himself—Have I valued the soul of this my child more than his body, his health, or any earthly advantage that I may lawfully have wished for him? Now that his worldly hopes are well nigh cut off, can I say that his eternal interest in Christ has been the chief desire of my heart? Has my conduct and example, have my words and counsels, and my daily intercourse with him, been such as to help him towards the attainment of everlasting glory? Can I appeal to him for the truth of this— that long before I apprehended danger to his life, I was above all things anxious to be well assured of his conversion—that I coveted this blessing, that I sought it, and laboured for it?

2. Turning to God, the parent may say—Lord, thou knowest all things, and there is no dissembling with thee. Thou knowest how feeble and how imperfect have been my best exertions and prayers for the salvation of this dear child, who now appears stricken for death. I must in truth confess, that I have sought the greatest of all blessings far too coldly; nay, even with a divided heart. Justly may I mourn, to think that I have been training him up too much for this life—too little for Thee! Yet, O Lord, I trust it hath been my ruling desire —as it is now—that he should be thine, here and

hereafter. Oh, let us not be separated from each other at the Last Day; but may we meet for ever at thy right hand! Thou seest and hearest my tears, my sighs, my prayers, on his behalf. Oh, forgive me, whereinsoever I have neglected or failed in the greatest of all duties to my child: forgive, O Lord; and prevent or repair the evil. Let thy good Spirit assist me, in this my need, to speak to the edification of one so dear to me. Lord, shut not thy merciful ears to my prayer. Give me the tongue of the learned, that I may be enabled, morning and noon and evening, to speak a word in season to him that is weary. Lord, open his heart, to receive instruction and comfort.

3. As for the sufferer, what it may be proper to say to him, must depend on a variety of circumstances: only a few general thoughts can here be offered. We may inquire—

— Has the Spirit of God been secretly working on your heart? Or are you, as yet, unconverted?

— What outward evidences are there, that a saving change hath been wrought in you?

— Is sin brought to your remembrance? Do you mourn for it with a godly sorrow?

— Are you convinced of the utter depravity of your natural heart; its vileness, weakness, blindness, and alienation from God?

— Have you discovered any particular corruption of your nature; and are you seeking grace to resist and subdue it?

— Do you study the Holy Scriptures, with self-application and self-examination? Are you accustomed to private prayer? Have you frequented the Lord's Table?

— Have you that faith, which alone can keep the soul at rest; the sure belief that Christ Jesus came into the world to save sinners, even the chief?

— Is your faith a living faith? Does it work by love?

— Has this love the true marks; namely, hatred of sin; a loathing of yourself; the subduing of your corruptions; delight in contemplating Christ's work; glorying in the Cross of Christ; renouncing all confidence in your own righteousness; love of the image of Christ when seen in others; desire that all men may be brought savingly to know him? In a word—When Jesus, who is altogether lovely, inquires into the state of your heart, can you answer plainly, " Lord, thou knowest all things; thou knowest that I love thee?"

Such are the inquiries which a Parent ought to make—such his topics of conversation, when watching over a dying child. Others might be suggested: but these are a few; and they are among the weightiest.

Let them be pressed tenderly—firmly—wisely—perseveringly.

Oh! how should Parents strive, while their children are in health, to lead them to the one thing needful! In the trying hour of separation, all the proofs that can be had, of their being in a state of grace, will be none too many. And if, at their departure, they leave a bright evidence of their having been made meet for glory, with what unspeakable joy shall we reflect that we faithfully offered them to God, and that He has graciously accepted them! They are gathered " as wheat into the garner!"

PRAYER.

Almighty and Eternal Lord God, with whom one day is as a thousand years, and a thousand years as one day: We bow down before thee, confessing ourselves poor and feeble creatures, fallen and miserable sinners, who depend entirely on thy pity, long-suffering, and goodness. We are but of yesterday, and know nothing; for our days on earth are a shadow. We are as a wind that passeth away and cometh not again.

O Lord, how often dost thou remind us of our frail and perishing condition! Thou callest away the grey-headed and aged, the infant and suckling: and when thou sendest abroad the messengers of death, the youngest and the strongest have no power to withstand thy sovereign will. Thou, even thou, art to be feared: and who may stand in thy sight, when once thou art angry?

We beseech thee, O Lord, to look graciously upon thy servants; and, in all our trials and sorrows, strengthen us by thy holy word; that we through patience and comfort of the Scriptures may have hope. Oh that thy word may be to us the joy and rejoicing of our heart: may we esteem it more than our necessary food. Give us grace to speak of it continually to our children while they are yet in health: write thy law in our heart and in theirs, that it may be our companion at all seasons, when we sit in the house, or walk by the way; when we lie down, and when we rise up. Unite us in the bonds of the everlasting Covenant, by faith in Christ, our living Head: and shed abroad in our hearts, and in the hearts of all who are dear to us, the grace of the Holy Ghost the Comforter: so that, whenever thou shalt be pleased to call any member of our families hence, we may have joy in the assurance that they sleep in Jesus, and are for ever with the Lord.

Lord, prepare the minds of those, whom thou hast appointed unto death, that they may be found ready when death shall come. Enable them to search and try their ways, and turn to thee with renewed repentance, and godly sorrow for sin. Let not any veil of ignorance, or of self-deceit, rest on their hearts. See if there be any wicked way in them: and lead them to know and embrace the Saviour with a true heart, and with full assurance of faith. Let thy Holy Spirit work in them that which is well-pleasing in thy sight: and receive them at length into thine everlasting kingdom.

We humbly commend to thy mercy, O Lord, ourselves and all belonging to us; beseeching thee to do for them and for us more than we are able to ask or think, according to the riches of thy grace, through Jesus Christ: to whom be glory in the Church, throughout all ages, world without end. Amen.

XXXI.
SOLOMON PRAYING FOR WISDOM.
1 Kings iii. 5—15.

In Gibeon the Lord appeared to Solomon in a dream by night: and God said, Ask what I shall give thee.

And Solomon said, Thou hast shewed unto thy servant David, my father, great mercy, according as he walked before thee in truth, and in righteousness, and in uprightness of heart with thee; and thou hast kept for him this great kindness, that thou hast given him a son to sit on his throne, as it is this day.

And now, O Lord my God, thou hast made thy servant king, instead of David my father: and I am but a little child: I know not how to go out or come in.

And thy servant is in the midst of thy people which thou hast chosen, a great people, that cannot be numbered nor counted for multitude.

Give therefore thy servant an understanding heart to judge thy people, that I may discern between good and bad: for who is able to judge this thy so great a people?

And the speech pleased the Lord, that Solomon had asked this thing.

And God said unto him, Because thou hast asked this thing, and hast not asked for thyself long life; neither hast asked riches for thyself, nor hast asked the life of thine enemies; but hast asked for thyself understanding to discern judgment;

Behold, I have done according to thy words: lo, I have given thee a wise and an understanding heart; so that there was none like thee before thee, neither after thee shall any arise like unto thee.

And I have also given thee that which thou hast not asked, both riches and honour: so that there shall not be any among the kings like unto thee all thy days.

And if thou wilt walk in my ways, to keep my statutes and my commandments, as thy father David did walk, then I will lengthen thy days.

WHEN we have any great duty before us—when we are entering, for example, upon any new situation in life, or any post of difficulty—it will be very serviceable for us to remember Solomon's prayer, and to make it our own : " Give me wisdom." Let this be the first, and the constant desire of our heart!

But it is not this petition alone that deserves our notice: the whole passage is worthy of our most attentive consideration.

1. The first thing to be noticed, is, the Thankfulness of heart which he manifests when stirring up his heart to pray. He *begins* with Praise,—praise for favours already received. He acknowledges the great goodness which God had shown to his father David, and to himself. Truth and righteousness had flourished under the reign of his father; and he himself was now securely placed on the throne. These were unspeakably great benefits, for which both himself and his people had cause to rejoice.—In like manner, whenever *we* approach the throne of grace in prayer for new blessings, we shall do well to thank God for the past. Let us heartily bless Him for former loving-kindnesses, and then ask for more.

2. The Humility of mind with which Solomon prays, is not less remarkable than his gratitude. He uses the lowliest words possible, to express his sense of his own ignorance and insufficiency. " I am but a little child: I know not how to go out, or how to come in." And he adds, " Who is able to judge this thy so great a people?"—meaning, " Surely I am not!"—Humility is one chief requisite in acceptable prayer. When we take a high

view of our duties, and a low view of our abilities, and when with these feelings we ask of God grace according to our necessities, we are welcome petitioners. " For God resisteth the proud, but giveth grace unto the humble."

3. The Faith also of Solomon is greatly to be admired. He was strong in faith, and therefore bold in prayer. No sooner does the Lord invite him in those words, " Ask what I shall give thee," than he immediately asks. The Spirit of grace and of supplication being poured out upon him, he does not hesitate or doubt: he takes God at his word: he asks, and he obtains.

St. James, when exhorting us to pray for this same gift, the gift of wisdom, adds the command, to " pray in faith, nothing wavering." When a Christian allows his faith to waver, then, the Apostle adds, " Let not that man think that he shall obtain any thing of the Lord."

4. Solomon's petition was itself characterized by that very wisdom for which he prayed. If he had not been already in some degree truly wise—and if he had not already felt the blessedness of being so— he would not have asked for wisdom in so prompt a manner. He had already tasted of the heavenly gift; and therefore coveted it the more earnestly. It is a mark of sound understanding to discern, at once, what it is that we most need, and what will be the most valuable to us.

How few possess this sound understanding!— Consider, for a moment, what it is that mankind generally desire. If men had a window in their breast, at which we could look in, and see the thoughts and wishes passing inside, should we not find the greater part of our fellow-creatures eagerly bent on those very things, which Solomon entirely left out of his prayer? "Oh, for long life, health, and enjoyment!" "Money, money by all means!" "Oh, that my enemy, or my rival, were put out of the way!"—these are the eager wishes of the many. What multitudes bargain away their immortal souls—and all for vanity!

5. The prayer of Solomon manifested also the greatest good-will toward others, especially his subjects. He was considering, not so much his own advantage, as the welfare of a great multitude, who were dependent on him. In praying for wisdom, he sought the happiness of the many thousands of Israel. It was the prayer, therefore, of an enlarged, benevolent, and disinterested heart. It was noble, generous, kingly.

Perhaps you may be ready to say—"But what good can *I* do? I am not a king." My friend, we all of us should aim at doing some good. Have we five talents? Let us make with them other five. Have we only one talent? Let us not hide it in a napkin.

Let us moreover remember this—that to govern well our own souls, to manage our worldly business, our families, and all our affairs with our fellow-creatures, is a work requiring much wisdom. You have not perhaps a large sphere: it may be well for you if you have not. But thus much is always within our reach—to learn and labour to get our own living, and to do our duty in that state of life unto which it hath pleased God to call us.

6. In a word, the prayer of Solomon shows that the Spirit of holiness ruled in his heart. It is said concerning him, that " Solomon loved the Lord, walking in all the statutes of David his father." This was then his character. He prayed, therefore, like one devoted to the glory of God, and to the good of his Church.

The Lord answered his prayer far beyond his expectations. He not only gave him a wise and an understanding heart; but he gave him also riches and honour. Solomon was the wealthiest, as well as the wisest, of all the kings of Israel.

Let us, however, while thus admiring Solomon, remember the affecting lesson afterwards taught us by his fall. Wise and holy as he was, yet for a long season he gave himself up to all the follies of idolatry, and to many sinful lusts and pleasures. There is reason to believe that he repented, and that the Spirit of God was not utterly taken from him. But the glory of Solomon was darkly shaded by his sins. Our only perfect pattern of wisdom and purity is the Lord Jesus Christ. Him we may not only admire, but trust: him we are bound to love, obey, and imitate, with all our heart and soul, and mind and strength. He it was who gave to Solomon this wisdom, though Solomon for a season abused the gifts of God. To us he freely offers the same inestimable treasure: not indeed worldly wisdom, but that grace by which we may be made wise unto salvation. Glory then only in Christ; in his rich promises, his holy doctrine, his bright example. "A greater than Solomon is here!"

PRAYER.

Almighty and most merciful Father, who through thy Son, Jesus Christ, hast promised to give thy Holy Spirit to them that ask thee: Grant to us, that, being united to Christ by a living faith, we may ever receive out of his fulness grace sufficient for us, even grace for grace. Let the Spirit of the Lord rest on us, thy humble servants;—the Spirit of wisdom and understanding, the Spirit of counsel and might, the Spirit of knowledge and of the fear of the Lord.

We beseech thee to bestow on us that wisdom which is profitable to direct us in all our conversation with mankind; especially when we are called to new or difficult duties. Leave us not to the darkness of our own understandings, or to the pride of our own reasonings: but sanctify every power of our souls; and bestow on us singleness of heart, that we may seek to glorify thee both in will and deed. Let the love of Christ constrain us to labour for the good of others, and to maintain a holy fellowship with them that are of the household of faith. Strengthen us with might, by thy Spirit, in the inner man, that we may be enabled both to will and to perform whatever is pleasing in thy sight.

Keep us, we pray thee, from those sins which do most easily beset us. When we think we stand, cause us to take the greater heed lest we fall. Suffer us not to become wise in our own conceits. Of thy great mercy, O Lord, grant us the comfort of thy presence; and make us a blessing to others, as we pass through this sinful world.

Raise up, O Lord, in every class of society, faithful and able persons, to maintain Thy cause, and to do good in their generation. Endue our Sovereign, and all that are in authority, with heavenly grace, that they may rule thy people in truth and righteousness. Give to all governors and pastors of thy Church the wisdom that is from above,—the wisdom that is pure and peaceable, full of mercy and good fruits. Be gracious to the people of this land, and lead them in the paths of righteousness for thy Name's sake. May it please thee to have mercy upon all men. Let wisdom and knowledge be the stability of our times, and the fear of the Lord our treasure. Be thou the strength of salvation to thy Church: defend, guide, and bless every member of the same. Thou only art our Sun and Shield, our joy and glory, O thou Prince of Peace, Jesus Christ our Lord: to Thee, therefore, with the Father and the Holy Spirit, be ascribed all honour, might, majesty, and dominion, now and for ever. Amen.

XXXII.

ELIJAH AND THE WIDOW.

1 Kings xvii. 8—16.

And the word of the Lord came unto him, saying,

Arise, get thee to Zarephath, which belongeth to Zidon, and dwell there: behold, I have commanded a widow woman there to sustain thee.

So he arose and went to Zarephath. And when he came to the gate of the city, behold, the widow woman was there, gathering sticks: and he called to her, and said, Fetch me, I pray thee, a little water in a vessel, that I may drink.

And as she was going to fetch it, he called to her, and said, Bring me, I pray thee, a morsel of bread in thine hand.

And she said, As the Lord thy God liveth, I have not a cake, but an handful of meal in a barrel, and a little oil in a cruse: and, behold, I am gathering two sticks, that I may go in and dress it for me and my son, that we may eat it, and die.

And Elijah said unto her, Fear not; go and do as thou hast said: but make me thereof a little cake first, and bring it unto me, and after make for thee and for thy son.

For thus saith the Lord God of Israel, The barrel of meal shall not waste, neither shall the cruse of oil fail, until the day that the Lord sendeth rain upon the earth.

And she went and did according to the saying of Elijah: and she, and he, and her house, did eat many days.

And the barrel of meal wasted not, neither did the cruse of oil fail, according to the word of the Lord, which he spake by Elijah.

This beautiful story furnishes us with some lessons that are highly important to all: it also offers peculiar encouragements to those who know and serve the Lord. Let us meditate on the various particulars of the narrative.

1. First, we see how easily God can punish a whole nation, when their sins have stirred his anger. He can shut up the heavens, and withhold the rain necessary for the growth of corn. When he does so—(thus causing bread to be very scarce and very dear)—it is a signal to us, not to murmur or rebel, as sinners often do; but, to humble ourselves before the Lord.

2. With humiliation, however, we ought to unite thankfulness. We should reflect, what a mercy it is that God causes the earth to bring forth its fruit so constantly, year after year, in due season. Sinners provoke the Lord every day; and yet his mercies are not come utterly to an end.

3. This story may well teach us the duty of practising moderation. By his simple and self-denying habits of life, the prophet Elijah had learned how to bear hardships. All that he asks for, is, a little water to drink, and a morsel of breat to eat.—Let us aim at being contented with a little, and with very simple things; since we know not what may be coming on the earth, or what hardships we may be called to endure. In times of scarcity we shall learn the value of the plainest food.

4. We are next reminded, that we ought to be bountiful in giving to others. "God loveth a cheerful giver." In times of want, instead of holding back, we should be most ready to be bountiful. This poor widow and her son were in the greatest straits: it is not unlikely that they

had seen some of their neighbours perish by the famine; and the widow represents that they themselves were even hard at death's door. Yet, encouraged by the word of the Lord spoken by Elijah, she freely brought to the wayfaring prophet the morsel which she was making ready for herself and her son. She was a poor, yet liberal servant of the Lord.

Much good may be done in a poor neighbourhood, and in hard times, when all lend a helping hand. "If thou hast little, do thy diligence to give gladly of that little."

5. Again: we may learn from this story to trust in Providence. Little did the prophet and the widow expect to be such helpers to each other, till God ordained their meeting! We never know what good things may be preparing for those who patiently wait the Lord's time. Our extremity may prove to be God's opportunity.—The continuance of the meal and oil was plainly miraculous: such a supply we do not expect. Yet, where strict Christian economy is used, very often, if it please God, small means hold out for a long time; till, through his goodness, better days appear.

6. But chiefly let us with joy remember, that the grace of God is inexhaustible! Bread and water may fail; but the mercy of the Lord endureth for ever. "To the poor the Gospel is preached:" and if the poor are rich in faith, the Gospel will make them blessed in their souls here, and blessed beyond all they can conceive in the world to come.

"He that spared not his own Son, but delivered him up for us all, how shall he not with him also freely give us all things?" Pardon, and peace, and the spirit of holiness, are great blessings: these we may have at all times, and that plenteously. "I am come," saith Jesus, "that they might have life; and, that they might have it more abundantly." In the kingdom of grace there is no such thing as famine! The prophet must die: the widow and her son, after a while, must die: so, in our turn, must we also. But "he that believeth in Jesus, though he were dead, yet shall he live: and whoso liveth and believeth in him, shall never die."

PRAYER.

O Lord God, our Creator, Preserver, and continual Benefactor: We acknowledge thy great and undeserved goodness to us, and to all men. It is of thine abundant treasure that we partake day by day. Thou openest thy hand, and satisfiest the desire of every living thing.

Teach us, O Lord, to accept thy mercies with a thankful heart, and to use the bounties of thy providence with holy moderation. In whatsoever state we are, enable us to be therewith content. Dispose us also to be liberal, according to our ability. Bestow on us the mind which was in Christ Jesus; that it may be our delight to go about doing good; and that we may ever account it more blessed to give, than to receive.

Prepare us for whatever changes may be appointed for us; for we know not what a day may bring forth. Shouldest thou withhold, or take away from us, the good things of this life, yet leave us not destitute of those things which accompany salvation. Satisfy our souls with thy hid treasure; with righteousness, joy, and peace in the Holy Ghost. And when thou shalt call us hence, receive us to thine everlasting kingdom, through our Lord and Saviour, Jesus Christ. Amen.

XXIII.

THE WIDOW'S SON.

1 Kings xvii. 17—24.

And it came to pass after these things, that the son of the woman, the mistress of the house, fell sick; and his sickness was so sore. that there was no breath left in him.

And she said unto Elijah, What have I to do with thee, O thou man of God? art thou come unto me to call my sin to remembrance, and to slay my son?

And he said unto her, Give me thy son. And he took him out of her bosom, and carried him up into a loft where he abode, and laid him upon his own bed.

And he cried unto the Lord, and said, O Lord my God, hast thou also brought evil upon the widow with whom I sojourn, by slaying her son?

And he stretched himself upon the child three times, and cried unto the Lord, and said, O Lord my God, I pray thee' let this child's soul come into him again!

And the Lord heard the voice of Elijah ; and the child's soul came into him again, and he revived.

And Elijah took the child, and brought him down out of his chamber into the house, and delivered him unto his mother: and Elijah said, See, thy son liveth.

And the woman said to Elijah, Now by this I know that thou art a man of God, and that the word of the Lord in thy mouth is truth.

How tender is the affection which a mother bears to her offspring! and how greatly must this be increased in a widow towards her only son! Yet sometimes our Heavenly Father, who is infinitely wise, sees fit to separate dearest relatives, by the stroke of death. When he does so, some of the lessons to be learned are the following.

1. First, a season of affliction is a time for calling our sins to remembrance. Humiliation before God is our duty always: yet times of sorrow are peculiarly suited to revive and strengthen our humbling recollections. It is not said what particular sin this widow-woman remembered. If afflictions make us thoughtful, we may easily call to mind many things, by which we have offended God, and grieved his Holy Spirit.

2. Should one of our children or beloved friends be sick, nigh unto death, we should commend that child, or that friend, to God; begging our Ministers and fellow-Christians to pray for his recovery. If his sickness becomes "so sore, that there is no breath left in him," it would be foolish in us to expect a miracle to raise him from the dead. We must needs leave him in the hands of the great and holy Judge; and we should ourselves prepare to meet our God, not knowing how soon our turn may come.

3. But what is there terrible in death, to those

who faithfully follow Christ? Nothing:—in their case, the sting of death is quite taken away. "They sleep in Jesus, and are blest." Even this widow, who perhaps had not much knowledge—(certainly not so much knowledge as we may enjoy under the Gospel dispensation)—yet believed that Elijah was the servant of God, and that the word of the Lord by his mouth was truth. How much more, then, may we take comfort from the words of Christ! He promises—"I will receive you unto myself, that where I am, there ye may be also."

4. How faithful and earnest should parents be, watching over the souls of their young children, and bringing them up in the nurture and admonition of the Lord! If our labours for the good of their souls are successful, then are we blessed indeed! Especially, should any one of them die in the Lord early, it will be our comfort to know that the beloved child is only gone home a little before us. The cold grave is his bed: but at the last day that body shall rise again, to be united as a glorious body to his departed spirit; while that spirit even now rests sweetly on the bosom of Jesus.

PRAYER.

O Lord God Almighty, merciful and gracious, slow to anger, and plenteous in mercy: Like as a father pitieth his children, so dost Thou pity them that fear thee. Thou dost not willingly afflict or grieve the children of men. But thou art a holy God, declaring thy displeasure against sin, by the judgments which thou dost execute. Thou hast set our iniquities before us, our secret sins in the light of thy countenance. When thou hidest thy face, we are troubled: when thou takest away our breath, we die and return to our dust.

Lord, we desire to humble ourselves under thy mighty hand. We are miserable, poor, and helpless sinners. There is in us no good thing: our very righteousnesses are defiled with sin, and we are utterly unworthy to approach thee, the holy and righteous God. But we come in the name of Him who is worthy, and who ever liveth at thy right hand, to make intercession for us. For Christ's sake pardon all that is amiss: forgive us all our sins, negligences and ignorances; and blot them out of the book of thy remembrance.

In all time of our affliction, bestow on us more of that broken and contrite heart, which thou wilt not despise. Increase our faith in thee, and comfort us by a more close communion with thee, through the Spirit. Sanctify all our troubles to the good of our souls.

Look graciously upon our families, our friends and neighbours; and supply all our wants, according to the riches of thy goodness. Thou knowest what is needful and best for us: have compassion upon our infirmities and necessities: leave us not, neither forsake us, O God of our salvation. Feed us with food convenient for us: but above all, nourish our souls with the Bread of eternal life. Guide us in safety through this wilderness below, and bring us finally to the land of everlasting rest, where thy servants are exalted to serve thee with joy unspeakable and full of glory, through Christ our Lord. Amen.

XXXIV.
HEARTINESS IN SERVING GOD.
2 Chronicles xxxi. 20, 21

And thus did Hezekiah throughout all Judah, and wrought that which was good and right and truth in the sight of the Lord.

And in every work that he began in the service of the house of God, and in the law, and in the commandments, to seek his God, he did it with all his heart, and prospered.

From this account of king Hezekiah, I propose to draw your attention to several religious duties. Since half-hearted persons cannot hope for success in any thing, may the Spirit of God stir up our wills and affections, to do whatsoever our hand findeth to do, zealously and with good courage!

1. Let me however, in the very first place, offer this question for your consideration—Have you reason to believe that your soul is really converted to God? If there be any ground for doubt on this point, then Conversion is that which you have before all things, and above all things, to labour for; God calls you to turn from sin, to seek pardon through faith in his Son Jesus Christ, and to enter on a life of holiness, by the promised help of his Spirit. Oh then, if this work has yet to be begun in you, let it be begun immediately: it is "the one

thing needful." And set about it in earnest: for it is not a light thing; it is your life.

2. But, if you be converted, yet conscience possibly may point out to you some great evil in your heart and life, which needs Correction. If so, correct that evil without delay. Let Reform begin at home—in your own soul. Allow of no neglect. Spare no sin, no lust, no evil habit, no favourite indulgence. Cut off the right hand; pluck out the right eye. Be faithful to conscience and to God, giving up whatever you know to be wrong in your course. Do this with all your heart, and prosper.

3. Let me take a particular instance.—Is there some Family Duty, which needs your attention? Perhaps Family Prayer; or Family Discipline; or the teaching the Children or Servants, training them to prayer, to public worship and to the study of the Holy Scriptures. When these home-duties have been long neglected, it requires some courage to set them up. Hezekiah had a whole kingdom to reform! Let Heads of Families see what they have to do in the smaller circle of their own households. And when convinced what their duty is, let them do it with all their heart, and prosper.

4. Have you to give special Advice or Reproof— possibly to some one nearly connected with you— a son, a servant, a friend, or a companion? Possibly, to a backslider from the service of God. This is a delicate office, but a most necessary one. " Thou shalt in any wise reprove thy brother, and

not suffer sin to rest upon him." Part of the difficulty lies in this—we find it no easy matter by gentleness to *win* upon him. But our main trial is to muster up courage *to be faithful.* No doubt Hezekiah had his share of difficulties in this respect. He discharged his duty, however, with unflinching firmness. Like him, having prayed for the graces of wisdom and kindness, let us aim at giving counsel or censure, where it is necessary; and let us do it with all our heart. Through God's blessing, we shall often prosper, far beyond our expectations.

5. It may be there is some great and good Public Work going on in the world, or in the Church; and you are called to bear some part in it. In such a case, lay aside all self-seeking, all self-importance, all self-indulgence. Publicity often tempts men to vain-glory. In working for God, we should take special care to do that, and that only, which is "good and right and truth before the Lord our God." We should act conscientiously, and with a pure heart. Looking therefore to his Blessed Spirit, to sanctify our motives, let us in the strength of the Lord lay hold on our portion of the work.—Let us do it with all our heart, and prosper.

6. These considerations will prepare us for the opposition of a sinful world. Whoever strives to mend the character of his neighbours, will certainly encounter enmity and ill-will. But in this respect we are not a whit worse off than king Hezekiah

was. When, in the course of his great national reformation, he sent messengers from city to city, inviting all Israel to repentance, many persons of different tribes mocked at his messengers, and laughed them to scorn. Trials such as these are permitted by God; but they ought not to discourage us. If we serve him with full purpose of heart, he can silence our enemies, and raise us up friends: and this he *will* do, for the glory of his own Name.

PRAYER.

Blessed Lord, who hast committed unto each of thy servants his several talents, and commanded us to occupy till thou come: Stir up, we beseech thee, our wills and affections, that we may glorify thee, and that, while we have opportunity, we may do good unto all men. We have a great work to do, and little time to do it in: O quicken us, while it is called to-day. Make us valiant for the truth upon the earth. Guide us with sound knowledge and understanding, that we may wisely design, and effectually execute, whatsoever our hand findeth to do in thy service, and for the benefit of our fellow-creatures.

O Thou, who workest in thy people both to will and to do, of thy good pleasure: Inspire us with earnest longings after those things which make for our spiritual and eternal profit. Cause us to work out our salvation with fear and trembling. Dispose us to wait on thee in continual prayer, and to obey thee with our whole heart. Give us grace to endure hardness, to deny ourselves, and to take up our cross daily and follow Christ. Pardon our many sins, and let thy blessing rest upon us, and upon our labours; that we may at all times enjoy thy favourable acceptance of us, through Jesus Christ, our Mediator and Redeemer. Amen.

XXXV.

HEZEKIAH, AFTER HIS SICKNESS.
2 Chronicles xxxii. 24—26.

In those days Hezekiah was sick to the death, and prayed unto the Lord: and he spake unto him, and gave him a sign.

But Hezekiah rendered not again according to the benefit done unto him; for his heart was lifted up: therefore there was wrath upon him, and upon Judah and Jerusalem.

Notwithstanding Hezekiah humbled himself for the pride of his heart, both he and the inhabitants of Jerusalem, so that the wrath of the Lord came not upon them in the days of Hezekiah.

While Hezekiah was greatly improving the condition of his kingdom, and at the very time that he "was magnified in the sight of all nations," it pleased God to visit him with a severe and dangerous illness. To prepare his mind for the worst, the prophet Isaiah was sent to him with this solemn message—"Set thine house in order; for thou shalt die, and not live." Hezekiah, agonized with pain, and overwhelmed with grief, immediately poured out his soul in strong crying and tears unto God. So effectual were his prayers, that the Lord spared him. Isaiah was sent again with a very different message:—"Thus saith the Lord, the God of David thy father, I have heard thy prayer, I have seen thy tears: behold, I will heal thee: on the third day thou shalt go up unto the House of the Lord." A sign also was given, to confirm this promise: the shadow on the sun-dial went back ten degrees.

On this occasion Hezekiah wrote a most affecting hymn, describing the anguish of his sickness, and the joy of his recovery. It is given in the prophecy of Isaiah, chap. xxxviii.: and if there had been no other memorial of Hezekiah's feelings, we should have concluded that he passed the rest of his days serving God consistently. The sacred historian, however, relates that it was otherwise with him.

Not long after, the king of Babylon sent ambassadors, partly to congratulate Hezekiah on his recovery, and partly to inquire concerning the wonder that was done in the land. What an excellent opportunity was this for instructing them in the nature of the True God! How, then, did Hezekiah receive them? What is related of his conduct is this:—" And Hezekiah hearkened unto them, and showed them all the house of his precious things, the silver, and the gold, and the spices, and the precious ointment, and all the house of his armour, and all that was found in his treasures: there was nothing in his house, nor in all his dominion, that Hezekiah showed them not." He seems to have received them somewhat in the spirit of a man of the world. They left Jerusalem impressed with ideas of his magnificence; but probably with very faint religious admonitions, if any.

In the sacred page, two sins are distinctly charged on Hezekiah—Pride and Ingratitude. It is said, "His heart was lifted up:" and, "Hezekiah rendered not again according to the benefit done unto him." His yielding thus to two of the most hateful of all sins—(hateful both to God and man)—may well amaze us. What warning ought we to take from the case of Hezekiah?

1. First, see the great danger of worldly prosperity. Our corrupt hearts are almost sure to be injured by it. Riches, and all that can be procured by riches, all the comforts, luxuries, pomps, and compliments of worldly men—are but so many snares to the soul. They tend to draw the heart from God, and fill us with self-importance: they increase the means of self-indulgence: and thus, they often bring down wrath from heaven on us or on our families. Therefore, covet them not, if you are without them: if you have them, abuse them not.

2. The deceitfulness and treacherousness of the heart are clearly seen in Hezekiah's case. That a man so full of tender and holy love to God in his sick chamber, should thus forget his vows—that one who owed so much to God, should let slip the opportunity of glorifying God, and be pleased with honour shown to himself—all this would appear incredible, did we not find our own hearts continually prone to the very same evils.

The design of God with Hezekiah was, "to try him, that he might know all that was in his heart." The evil was all there, beforehand: but Hezekiah suspected it not.—Could we view all the evil of our nature, we should see that Ingratitude and Pride have very deep roots in our heart.

3. This story enforces also the duty of praying that God would never for a moment leave us to ourselves. It is said concerning Hezekiah, that "God left him, to try him." He left him, not intending finally to cast him off; but to show him that he was not safe for an instant, if he did not continue "watching unto prayer." Let us then "pray without ceasing:" for we need the aid of God's Holy Spirit continually. Especially let us be on our guard when returning from the dark chamber of sickness into the broad sunshine of health and activity.

4. For our comfort, we learn, however, that there is pardoning and restoring grace for the penitent. Without this, the case of Hezekiah would have been mournful indeed! But it is related, that "he humbled himself for the pride of his heart." Far better, had he never yielded to pride: but having indulged that sin, it was well that he did not persist in it. The Lord, therefore, in mercy spared him. Our Redeemer is ever ready to receive us back again to his favour, when we bewail our follies with godly sorrow and shame.

PRAYER.

O Almighty God, in whose hand is our breath, and whose are all our ways: We acknowledge thy great goodness towards us, by which we have been preserved alive unto this day.

We adore thee above all for thine unspeakable love, in the redemption of the world by our Lord Jesus Christ. We bless thee for all the rich promises of grace which thou hast made, in Him, to us miserable sinners.

But, O Lord, we confess with shame, that we have not been duly thankful for thy manifold mercies bestowed on us. When we were in trouble, we poured out our complaint before thee. Thou wast very gracious unto us at the voice of our cry: and thou hast spared us to serve and glorify thee a little longer on earth. But, oh! how do our treacherous hearts go back to the world! We forget the tender compassions of our Saviour: our affections grow cold, and we are unmindful of those consolations of the Spirit which upheld us when we were sinking. We soon decline from that meek and lowly frame of heart, which sometimes we feel while thy chastening rod is upon us.

O Lord, unto thee belong mercies and forgivenesses; but unto us belongeth confusion of face. Justly mightest thou punish us for our ingratitude and pride; but we beseech thee, deal not with us after our sins. Correct us in measure; not in thine anger, lest thou bring us to nothing. Humble us at the sight of our vileness. Show to us more clearly our weakness and insufficiency. Keep us steadfast in thy covenant: stablish and uphold us by thy free Spirit. Speak peace, Lord, to thy servants: but let us not turn again to folly. Enable us to walk circumspectly, and to pass the time of our sojourning here in fear. Give us grace so to honour thy great name before men, and so to live to thy praise, that when thou shalt call us hence, we may have comfort in the assurance of thy favour: and being found of thee in peace, may we have an abundant entrance ministered to us, into thine everlasting kingdom, through Christ our Lord. Amen.

XXXVI.

SORROW FOR NATIONAL SINS.

Ezra ix. 4—6.

Then were assembled unto me every one that trembled at the words of the God of Israel, because of the transgression of those that had been carried away; and I sat astonied until the evening sacrifice.

And at the evening sacrifice I arose up from my heaviness; and having rent my garment and my mantle, I fell upon my knees, and spread out my hands unto the Lord my God,

And said, O my God, I am ashamed and blush to lift up my face to thee, my God: for our iniquities are increased over our head, and our trespass is grown up unto the heavens.

To confess our sins before God, is evidently a duty, in order to our obtaining forgiveness. But there is one important consideration generally overlooked. When sin is mentioned, many only regard what they, simply considered in themselves, have done amiss: they do not reflect how far they share in the guilt of others, or how far they may have contributed to the sins of their family, their neighbourhood, or their country. They look at themselves as standing alone, not as members of society.

Ezra took a larger view of this subject. On discovering the sins committed by many of his fellow-countrymen, he laid the matter to heart, as affecting himself and the whole nation.

Suffer me to show you, how you may have contributed to the sinfulness of others.

1. First, reflect, whether you have not, at various times in your life, kept company with others in sin. Sometimes you were the tempted party: at other times, were you not the tempter? Sometimes you have sinned with one or with a few: at other times you have gone after a multitude to do evil. However the case may be in these respects, is it not certain, that you and they together have added to the sins of the nation? Have you not increased the number of sinners, and the amount of sin?

2. If you have been kept back from very gross crimes, yet possibly you have not unwillingly been amused with the sins of others. Have you smiled at the ridiculous attitudes of the drunkard, at the low wit of profane people, or the indecent jests and songs of the profligate? How much then have you sinned, by countenancing sin in others!

3. Consider, now, that one great duty—the sanctification of the Lord's Day. It has much, very

much, to do with all our other duties, and with God's blessing on a nation. How have you spent that day? Was it in worldly business, or in idle visiting and pleasure-taking? If this be in any measure your case, have you not increased that crying sin of our land, Sabbath-breaking?

4. Again—Look into your family; look at children and servants; or look among your nearest connections, your partners in business, and the persons actually in your employment:—what proof have you of your dealing faithfully with them? Have you increased the general iniquity; or have you checked it? Whom have you warned? Whom have you taught? Whom have you reproved? Whom have you counselled? With whom have you pleaded for God? Whom have you stirred up to care for their immortal souls?—Do not these questions remind you of your innumerable sins of omission? While neglecting these duties, have you not partaken in the public guilt?

5. Remember, that even by our secret transgressions we may, sooner or later, bring misery, not on ourselves only, but also on others. When Achan sinned, Israel was smitten: (Joshua vii.) Nay more: by our secret neglect of duty, we may draw down wrath from heaven. For example, by omitting private prayer, we do, as far as lies with us, rob others of those blessings which God was ready to bestow on them, had we earnestly interceded on their behalf.

You see, my friend, that we are answerable for

much more than many persons suppose. Let us not hide from ourselves our share in the guiltiness of our Church and Nation. Like Ezra, let us blush: like him and the saints of his company, let us tremble and be in heaviness, and spread out our hands unto the Lord our God, entreating him to spare, to pity, and to forgive.

But let me add this consideration.—If our heart be right with God, not only shall we cry and sigh for all the evil around us; but we shall strive to put down sin, and to promote holiness. To this end, we must labour, not in our own strength, but in the strength of the Lord, and in the power of his might.

Sometimes you may be ready to complain—" The world is so very corrupt, that little can be done to amend it—scarcely any thing at all!" But, oh be not disheartened. God can work by one poor wise man, to the saving of a whole city: (Eccl. ix. 13—15.) And, though much will always remain undone, still be encouraged by remembering, that should you gain one soul to God, THAT ONE SOUL is of greater value than thousands of worlds. When we labour and pray for the souls of men, we are working for Eternity!

PRAYER.

O Lord, thou Governor among the nations: Thine eyes are in every place, beholding the evil and the good. We bow down before Thee, and humble ourselves on account of our manifold transgressions, whereby we have provoked Thee to anger. How have we broken Thy holy law, abused our religious privileges, slighted thine ordinances, and neglected thy great salvation!

We remember to our unspeakable shame, that we have often tempted others to sin, or have taken pleasure in those who did evil. We have joined hand in hand, and hardened one another against thy fear. And now our iniquities are grown up unto the heavens, and we have just cause to dread lest wrath should come upon us to the uttermost.

We beseech thee, O Lord, to waken our consciences, that we may not continue in sin, and that iniquity may not be our ruin. For thy dear Son's sake, pardon, good Lord, and spare us: and henceforth put thy fear into our hearts, and write thy laws in our minds. Look in mercy upon our families and friends, upon our neighbours and all the people of this land. Recover us from every evil path, and lead us in the way everlasting.

Purify, establish and enlarge thy Church, both in this land, and throughout the whole world. Pour forth of thy Spirit upon all flesh, that there may be a reviving of thy work of grace among all nations. Hear the prayers of those who earnestly desire that sinners may be converted unto thee. Though iniquity abounds, let not the love of thy servants wax cold: but make them steadfast, unmoveable, always abounding in the work of the Lord.

We ask the forgiveness of our sins, and thy gracious acceptance of us, and of our poor imperfect prayers and services, for the sake of Jesus Christ, our Lord and our Redeemer. Amen.

XXXVII.
THE PATIENCE OF JOB.
Job i. 20—22.

Then Job arose, and rent his mantle, and shaved his head, and fell down upon the ground, and worshipped,

And said, Naked came I out of my mother's womb, and naked shall I return thither: the Lord gave and the Lord hath taken away; blessed be the name of the Lord.

In all this Job sinned not, nor charged God foolishly.

WELL might St. James say, as speaking of a matter known to the whole Church of God—"Ye have heard of the patience of Job!" Wonderful, beyond all other history, is the Scripture account of the sufferings and the faith of this holy man.

In this chapter we read of his losing, first, all his sheep, camels, and servants, by the violence of robbers and murderers, who suddenly came on them, and carried away all his substance. Next, —and bitterest of all!—his ten children (that is, seven sons and three daughters) were, without a moment's warning, cut off from the land of the living. As they were visiting in the house of the eldest brother, " there came a great wind from the wilderness, and smote the four corners of the house, and it fell upon the young men:"—the messenger then adds, " And they are dead: and I only am escaped to tell thee."

The next chapter relates, that Satan was permitted yet further to try this upright servant of the Lord. Job was tormented with a sore disease, which made him a burden to himself, while his whole body became offensive to others. His wife, who was like "one of the foolish women," soon lost her patience; and instead of soothing her husband, as she ought to have done, advised him to give up life in despair. She said, "Curse God and die:" suggesting, that he might as well make away with himself at once. How mild, yet how wise and holy was his answer! After rebuking her, he meekly adds, "Shall we receive good at the hands of the Lord, and shall we not receive evil?"

Returning to the account of his children's death, we may observe two remarkable points in the language which he uttered on hearing of that awful event. One part of his words has reference to himself; the other, to the Lord.

1. Of himself he speaks most humbly. He notices the periods of his birth and of his death; the beginning and the end of his short span of life. "Naked came I out of my mother's womb, and naked shall I return thither." As though he had said—My mother, who bare me, beheld me a poor, naked, helpless infant: and when I return to my mother-earth, to the dust out of which I was taken, I shall be stripped of every thing: I shall again be just as poor and helpless a creature as I was at the moment of my birth: nay, even more so; for I shall be cold, motionless, lifeless.—His lan-

guage reminds us of the words of St. Paul, words so plain and undeniable: "We brought nothing into this world; and it is certain we can carry nothing out."

2. Concerning the Lord he speaks with submission and holy adoration. All his substance, all his family, had been snatched from him in one day: yet he murmurs not. He does not charge God foolishly: not a word escapes him expressive of a rebellious or repining heart. On the contrary, he says the very thing that he ought to say: and the words which he then uttered, have been used by thousands, as the best relief to hearts overwhelmed with anguish: "The Lord gave, and the Lord hath taken away: blessed be the name of the Lord!"

It is peculiarly touching to see how these words apply to what Job most delighted in; namely, his family:—a large grown-up family, which he had brought up religiously. "The Lord gave"—He it was who gave me these ten children: they were very dear to me, and I brought them up for Him. "The Lord hath taken away"—He hath cut them off in the vigour of their age: they are deprived of the residue of their years! I cannot but weep and mourn for them; and in falling down upon the ground, I cannot help thinking how soon the cold earth must cover them: and after a short space it will receive me also; the grave being "the house appointed for all living."— But I cannot open my mouth against the Lord! Oh no: He hath done all things well! With a bleeding heart, I can still adore his wisdom and his love: I can still say from my inmost soul, Blessed be the Name of the Lord!"

My friend, the history of Job may in some particulars be suitable to your case, or to the circumstances of those who are dear to you. Greater sorrows, or sorrows even equal to his, you scarcely can have felt or seen.—But what should you now do in your affliction! Oh, entreat the Lord that he would, by the power of his Holy Spirit, enable you to imitate the humility, the faith, the patience of this holy man. Like him, bow the head and worship. Remember the infinite love and pity of the Lord Jesus Christ. Go in prayer to him. He sits upon a throne of grace. He waits to see whether now, in the day of sorrow, you will come to him: and whether you will "cast all your care upon him, believing that he careth for you." Oh, draw near to him! In simple faith, cling to his footstool! If, through grace, you gain spiritual benefit from your trials, you will in the end say—as thousands of God's children have said before you—" It is good for me that I have been afflicted."

PRAYER.

O Lord God, full of compassion and gracious, long-suffering and plenteous in mercy and truth: Enable us, under every tribulation, to pour out our hearts before thee, and to trust in thee as our refuge and strength, a very present help in time of trouble. Subdue every proud and rebellious thought within us: conform us to thy blessed will, and cause us to rest in thy love.

Lord, we lament before thee our manifold and great infirmities, and we acknowledge the imperfection of all our graces. But do Thou, who layest the burden of affliction upon us, vouchsafe us also needful strength to bear it. Suffer us not to be weary of thy correction. Cheer us with the communion of the saints; and guide thy servants to speak to us what is wise and holy and comforting. But, above all, let our faith and hope be strengthened through the rich communications of thy Holy Spirit, who is the Teacher and Comforter of thy people. Let patience have her perfect work; and in all things enable us to glorify thy holy Name, both now and ever, through Jesus Christ, our merciful High Priest and Advocate; to whom, with Thyself and the Holy Spirit, be all praise and thanksgiving, world without end. Amen.

XXXVIII.
THE RESURRECTION OF THE DEAD.
Job xix 25—27.

For I know that my Redeemer liveth, and that he shall stand at the latter day upon the earth:

And though after my skin, worms devour this body, yet in my flesh shall I see God:

Whom I shall see for myself, and mine eyes shall behold, and not another; though my reins be consumed within me.

FROM various parts of Job's discourses, it is evident, that while his body was racked with disease, his mind also was in a most melancholy state. Hence he gives utterance to such mournful expressions as the following:—" My breath is corrupt, my days are extinct, the graves are ready for me." " I have said to corruption, Thou art my father; and to the worm, thou art my mother and my sister." But in the words now before us, there is a pleasing dignity. He speaks of the grave with calmness, because he looks far beyond it. He bequeaths his poor sickly body to the worms, triumphing to think that it shall be raised " a glorious body." His eye, soon to be extinguished in death, shall be lighted up again; and, face to face, for himself, shall he behold " the King in his beauty."

The words are a noble declaration of the doctrine of the Resurrection.

1. First, observe that the Patriarch prophetically speaks of Christ, under the glorious title, " My Redeemer."—What is this work of Redemption?

It may in few words be thus stated:—By nature we are slaves of sin, and children of wrath. By our actual sins also we have added to our guilt, and increased our curse. But Jesus, having paid the ransom, sets us free. " He died for our sins, and rose again for our justification:" and He now ever liveth at the right-hand of God, " to make intercession for us." Believing in Jesus, therefore, "we have redemption through His blood, even the forgiveness of sins." " Being justified by His blood, we shall be saved from wrath through Him."

2. This glorious Redeemer is described as the Lord of life. Job says of Him, "My Redeemer liveth." Although Christ had not as yet appeared on earth in the flesh, yet this enlightened patriarch knew that He existed, even from eternity. In like manner Christ spake concerning himself. He declared, "As the Father hath life in Himself, so hath He given to the Son to have life in Himself." He solemnly declares also, "I am the Resurrection and the Life." He is the same ever-living Saviour in all ages; the Saviour of Job, of Abraham, of Moses, of David, of all the Patriarchs, Prophets, Apostles and Martyrs. He is our Saviour, as well as theirs. Time makes no change in Him. He is "Jesus Christ, the same yesterday, and to-day, and for ever."

3. The Redeemer will hereafter appear in glory. "Christ is risen from the dead, and is become the first-fruits of those that sleep." In the day of the Resurrection, He will descend from heaven, "and before Him shall be gathered all nations." Then "every eye shall see Him." You and I shall then be summoned by Him to judgment.—Solemnly let us consider, Where shall we then appear? Shall we be found on His right-hand or on His left?

4. What support and comfort does this doctrine of the Resurrection give to a believer, under all his trials! He can view all his present "light afflictions" as working out for him "a far more exceeding and eternal weight of glory."—This it was that upheld the sinking heart of Job. Blessed

are they who, like him, can say, "I shall see God!" that is—I shall meet him in glory! I shall see my Redeemer, when he welcomes the righteous to the kingdom prepared for them from the foundation of the world: and I trust that through his merits, I shall, together with them, " enter into the joy of my Lord!"

Solemnly reflect again, my friend, Where will you then appear; on the right-hand, or on the left?

PRAYER.

O Eternal and Ever-blessed Redeemer, who art the Resurrection and the Life: We beseech thee, work in us the work of faith with power; and so unite us by thy Spirit to thyself, that, believing in thee, we may have life through thy name. Oh, that we may know thee, and the power of thy resurrection, and the fellowship of thy sufferings, being made conformable to thy death; daily dying to all carnal lusts, and mortifying the deeds of the body, and living unto God.

Lord, in this our earthly tabernacle we groan, being burdened with corruption and infirmity, with temptations and many troubles. O remember how short our time is! Spare us, that we may recover strength, before we go hence, and be no more. Quicken us to live to thy glory. Grant us the presence of thy blessed Spirit, to comfort our hearts, and stablish us in the hope of the Gospel.

Now the God of peace, that brought again from the dead our Lord Jesus, that great Shepherd of the sheep, through the blood of the everlasting covenant, make us perfect in every good work to do his will, working in us that which is well-pleasing in his sight, through Jesus Christ: to whom be glory for ever and ever. Amen.

XXXIX.
THE RIGHT SPIRIT FOR THE AFFLICTED.
Job xxxiv. 31, 32.

Surely it is meet to be said unto God, I have borne chastisement, I will not offend any more:

That which I see not, teach thou me: if I have done iniquity, I will do no more.

When we are tried by great afflictions, it is very difficult to settle down our hearts into a calm and holy frame. Losses sour the mind: bereavements sadden it: the spirit of contradiction irritates it: while pain and disease wear out the spirits, making us feel weary of almost every body and every thing. Nay, in such a state we are even tempted to have hard thoughts of God himself!

Thus it was with Job: but happily he had one kind and wise adviser, Elihu, who put, as it were, the language of confession and prayer into his lips; showing him in what posture of mind he should place himself before God.

From this suggestion of Elihu, let me show to *you*, my suffering friend, with what spirit of mind you should bear the chastening of the Lord.

1. First, seek to enjoy communion with God, by the Spirit, through Jesus, your compassionate Redeemer and Advocate. He can be touched with the feeling of your infirmities, having been in all points tempted like as you are, but without sin. Therefore in his Name speak to God. Cease from man: for, as to your fellow-creatures, some cannot understand you; others will not feel for you; and perhaps none of them can help you. But God knows already all the grief that is in your heart. Tell it to him: he can and will relieve you.

2. This will lead to Resignation. Remember, all chastisement comes from a kind Father. The rod, of whatever kind it may be, is held by his hand!— He will not lay upon man more than is right. We deserve it all, and more.—He does not afflict us for his own pleasure, but for our profit.—Reflect, too, that as we cannot escape his hand, it is best to wait for his time of deliverance. "Let patience have her perfect work." Pray as earnestly for submission as for deliverance.

3. A spirit of deep Humility is peculiarly called for in times of affliction. When, with so much tenderness, Elihu put this language into Job's mouth —"If I have done iniquity," he did not mean to express any doubt in the case: he rather reminded Job that a spiritual insight into his heart and life would soon show him depths of vileness there.

True humility is described in Scripture by the expressions, "a tender heart," "a broken spirit," "a broken and contrite heart." Other kinds of sorrow are—either selfish vexation—or a proud anger against God and hatred of him—or the inward gnawing of conscience without hope. But there is a godly sorrow, which "worketh repentance unto salvation, not to be repented of." The more we look to the Cross of Christ, the more shall we weep, and be in bitterness before the Lord, for all our sins, negligences, and ignorances.

This flow of penitence gives wonderful relief to an afflicted soul. It is like the bursting of a painful, inflamed ulcer. When with crying and tears we confess, " I have sinned," soon comes the healing words, " Thy sins be forgiven thee; go in peace."

4. Next, cultivate a spirit of Dutiful Obedience to the will of God. It is meet that the sinner, after lamenting his iniquity, should add, " I will do no more." But let this be a thorough renunciation of all sin; and let it be accompanied by the steady obedience of a willing heart, a watchful and diligent heart,—an obedience flowing, not from terror, but from the spirit of adoption. He that hath had much forgiven, will love much: and he that loves much, will serve joyfully.

5. Yet again, seek by prayer an increase of Teachableness. Having been taught something of your corruptions, and of the methods of Divine grace; having learned something of duty and of the love of Christ; you will find, nevertheless, that you are still only at the beginning of your lesson. We are like little children, making a few ill-shapen letters in their copy-book, and too soon delighted

with their performances. Repeated trials show us what poor scholars we are! Let us, therefore, go and sit again at the feet of Jesus, saying, "That which I see not, teach thou me."—Possibly God may judge it needful to send you new afflictions. Perceiving how little you have profited by the past, he seems to ask, "Have ye suffered so many things in vain—if it be yet in vain!" What should we then answer him? "Teach me, O thou Divine Master; teach me anew. Choose thine own method of teaching. Take my heart as it is: plough it: harrow it: sow it: water it: refresh it with the dew of thy Spirit: cause the Sun of righteousness to shine upon it:—only, make it fruitful!"

PRAYER.

O Lord God most holy, just and good: We have sinned; what shall we say unto thee, O Thou Preserver of men? But now, O Lord, thou art our Father: we are the clay, and thou our Potter; and we all are the work of thy hand. Be not wroth very sore, O Lord, neither remember iniquity for ever.

It is good that a man should both hope, and quietly wait for the salvation of the Lord. But we have too often been impatient under thy rod: we have been foolish and perverse in our spirit, and our heart hath often fretted against the Lord. Pardon, we pray thee, all the unseemly and unholy conduct, whereof we have so much reason to be ashamed. And, for the time to come, enable us to behave and quiet ourselves, as a child that is weaned of his mother: yea, let our soul be even as a weaned child.

O continue thy loving-kindness unto us, and teach us to do thy will, for thy Spirit is good. Make us more watchful and circumspect, more simple and sincere, more constant and devoted in thy service.

Now the God of hope fill us with all joy and peace in believing, that we may abound in hope, through the power of the Holy Ghost, for Jesus Christ's sake. Amen.

XL.

THE HUMILITY OF JOB.

Job xl. 3—5. and xlii. 5, 6.

Then Job answered the Lord, and said,

Behold, I am vile; what shall I answer thee? I will lay mine hand upon my mouth.

Once have I spoken; but I will not answer: yea, twice; but I will proceed no further.

* * * * *

I have heard of thee by the hearing of the ear: but now mine eye seeth thee

Wherefore I abhor myself, and repent in dust and ashes.

This is not the language of affected humility. Job was not an ignorant untried man: nor did he say more than he felt. And if Job so deeply abased himself, surely we have no reason to be proud.

Long before this, Job had known the Lord, and

had served him faithfully. But it pleased God, in a remarkable manner, to reveal Himself more fully to His servant. The design of God was, to bring him into a state of entire submission and deep self-abasement. When, by the power of his Holy Spirit, the Lord had wrought this work, Job viewed his former attainments in religion as being almost nothing, compared with those larger views which were now vouchsafed to him. Before, he had only "heard with the hearing of the ear: but now," he adds, "mine eye seeth thee."

The ear, though a quick organ, yet is dull when compared with the eye. The eye, moreover, is the most comprehensive of all our senses: it takes in the widest range of objects: things exceedingly distant pass into the mind, through the eye, in a moment.

The Lord frequently vouchsafes to his most favoured servants a very quick insight into things divine: but this penetrating view is always accompanied by the deepest feelings of self-abasement.

Consider, what are the thoughts which the Holy Spirit is wont thus to impress upon the soul.

1. First, the Almighty power of God is then deeply felt. Like Job, we cry out with awe, "I know that thou canst do every thing." How feeble are we, who " dwell in houses of clay, whose foundation is in the dust, which are crushed before the moth !"

2. The wisdom and knowledge of God are then acknowledged to be unsearchable. We feel that

we are more ignorant and foolish than children. Especially, the knowledge which God has of our most secret imaginations, is wonderful. " I know that no thought can be withholden from thee!" Who can escape such a Judge as this?

3. The perfect Equity of God's dealings is then perceived. We are plainly convicted of folly and presumption, for having ever entertained a single murmur against Him.—This was deeply felt by Job.

4. But the view of His holiness is what peculiarly abases his servants.—Let me illustrate this.

Imagine a person beholding his natural face in a glass: he thinks his appearance fair and respectable, his countenance sufficiently pleasant, his clothing decent and clean. But now suppose him to turn, and see near him a Glorious Being of more than angelic brightness; with eyes as a flame of fire, lips expressive of wisdom, hands busily engaged in works of mercy. Conceive him gazing long and earnestly upon this Person; and then turning again to survey his own countenance:— how will he now regard himself? Will he not appear vile and base in his own eyes; his hands, polluted; his garments, mean; nay, even as filthy rags? Comparing himself with that Glorious Person, he will be utterly unable to endure the sight of himself.

This may show you what a saint feels, when contemplating the holiness and purity of God. So long as he sees only his own supposed good works, and compares himself with himself, he fancies that he has somewhat whereof to boast. But when, with devout meditation, and with the eye of faith, he beholds the infinite holiness of God, then his heart sinks under the feeling of its own vileness. No language is too strong to describe the sense which he now has of his own unworthiness and guilt.

He now, therefore, adopts, as his own, all the expressions used by holy men of old—such as Job, Abraham, Isaiah, Ezra, and St. Paul—when speaking of their own vileness. "I am but dust and ashes." " Woe is me, for I am undone: for I am a man of unclean lips, and I dwell in the midst of a people of unclean lips, and mine eyes have seen the King, the Lord of Hosts." " O my God, I blush, and am ashamed to lift up my face unto thee." " I am the chief of sinners." " If I wash me with snow-water, and make my hands never so clean," (these are Job's own words,) " yet shalt thou plunge me in the ditch, and mine own clothes shall abhor me."

5. It is high time for us, however, to take that view which alone can sustain us, when overwhelmed by a sense of our vileness;—the view, I mean, of God's infinite love, revealed to us in Christ Jesus. This was fully seen, though it is not here expressed by Job: otherwise he must have sunk into despair. —And yet, while this love of God soothes the fainting spirit, it also humbles a believer more than any thing else can do. He is broken-hearted, when thinking of this amazing fact, " Jesus died for me!" Terror never lays him so low in his own eyes, as

a sight of the love of his Redeemer does. It is at the foot of the cross that he sighs forth most deeply "I am vile: I abhor myself!"

Let a short remark or two close the account of this eminent patriarch. If ever there was a history to establish this truth—" He that humbleth himself shall be exalted"—it is the history of Job. As soon as Job abased himself, God raised him up. The Lord makes him a priest, to offer up sacrifices on behalf of his three friends; comforts him on every side; carries him to a good old age, and crowns him with the richest blessings.

The venerable man lived, after this, one hundred and forty years. How would he delight in recounting to his sons, and his sons' sons, the wonderful deliverances which he had experienced: summing up his narrative with some such reflections as these—" I am the man that hath seen the goodness and the faithfulness of God. I have seen *the end of the Lord* in all his dealings toward me: and to my dying day will I testify, that the Lord is very pitiful and of tender mercy!"

PRAYER.

O God the Father, God the Son, and God the Holy Ghost: Have mercy upon us, miserable sinners! We acknowledge our wretchedness: we are sorry for our sins!

But oh, how little have we attained to the knowledge of Thy glory, and of our own vileness! How highly do we sometimes conceive of our own goodness, lightly regarding thy condescension to such miserable worms! We have proudly reasoned against thy dispensations, instead of submitting to them: we have sinned presumptuously, and provoked thine anger: we have carried ourselves irreverently in thy presence, O thou great God, who dost fill heaven and earth!

Lord God Almighty, when we remember who and what Thou art, and then view our own meanness and unworthiness, we are amazed at thy patience and forbearance and long-suffering towards us. But when we think upon the love of Christ, our souls are filled with shame and self-abhorrence, on account of our exceeding sinfulness and vileness in thy sight. Lord, what is man, that thou art mindful of him; and the son of man, that thou visitest him?

Grant, Lord, that looking unto Jesus, whom we have pierced, we may mourn and be in bitterness for our sins. O look upon us in pity, through Him: blot out all our unrighteousness with his atoning blood; and cover us with Thy righteousness, which is by faith of Jesus Christ, unto all and upon all them that believe.

What it may please thee to do with us in this mortal state, we know not, neither do we ask to know. But we beseech thee to have mercy upon our souls, and to grant us thy salvation. Cast us not away from thy presence; take not thy Holy Spirit from us. Lift up upon us the light of thy countenance. While we live, enable us to live to thy glory. When we die, may we die at peace with Thee, and with all men: and, being found in Christ, grant us a place at thy right-hand, where are pleasures for evermore.

Now unto Him that is able to keep us from falling, and to present us faultless before the presence of his glory with exceeding joy: To the only wise God our Saviour, be glory and majesty, dominion and power, both now and ever. Amen.

THE END.

BY THE SAME AUTHOR.

Third Edition, Price 3s. 6d. cloth:
THE CHRISTIAN VISITOR,
ON THE FOUR GOSPELS.

Second Edition, Price 3s. 6d. cloth:
THE CHRISTIAN VISITOR,
ON THE ACTS AND THE EPISTLES.

Price 3s. 6d. cloth:
THE CHRISTIAN VISITOR,
ON THE OLD TESTAMENT:
PART II.—PSALMS TO MALACHI.

Third Edition, enlarged, 3s. 6d. cloth:
TIME AND TEMPER,
SELECTIONS FROM SCRIPTURE, WITH REMARKS,
and Extracts from various English Authors:
ALSO—THOUGHTS ON EDUCATION.

Third Edition, 6s. 6d. cloth:
MEMOIR
OF THE
REV. CORNELIUS NEALE, M.A.
To which are added,
His REMAINS; being Sermons, Allegories, and various Compositions in Prose and Verse.

Price 1s. cloth:
THOUGHTS ON CONVERSION,
IN NINE LETTERS, ADDRESSED TO A YOUNG RELATIVE.

Price 5s. cloth:
HELPS TO PASTORAL VISITATION,
IN THREE PARTS.

Price 3s. 6d. cloth:
THE LAST DISCOURSE AND PRAYER
OF OUR LORD JESUS CHRIST
As recorded in St John's Gospel, Chap. xiii. to xvii.
WITH PRACTICAL REMARKS.

LONDON:
PRINTED BY WILLIAM WATTS,
Crown Court, Temple Bar.

WORKS RECENTLY PUBLISHED
BY SEELEY, BURNSIDE, AND SEELEY,
54 FLEET STREET.

Christian Biography.

A MEMOIR OF BISHOP CORRIE,
OF MADRAS;
With extracts from his Correspondence.
In one volume 8vo. Price 14s. cloth

THE LIFE AND LETTERS OF THE
REV. HENRY MARTYN.
In two volumes, with Engravings, price 6s. each, in cloth

THE LIFE OF DEAN MILNER.
By his NIECE
Abridged, in one Vol. foolscap. Price 6s cloth

MEMOIRS OF THE LIFE AND CORRESPONDENCE
OF MRS. HANNAH MORE.
Edited by W. ROBERTS, Esq. With Portrait.
Abridged In One Volume, Foolscap 8vo. Price 6s in cloth

A MEMOIR OF THE
REV. LEGH RICHMOND, M.A.
Rector of Turvey, Bedfordshire, &c
By the Rev T. S GRIMSHAWE, M.A.; Rector of Burton Latimer,
With a Portrait. Eleventh Edition. Foolscap 8vo. Price 6s in cloth.

MEMOIRS OF
THE LIFE OF W. WILBERFORCE, ESQ. M.P.
BY HIS SONS,
The Ven. ROBERT ISAAC WILBERFORCE, Archdeacon of E R. York
And the Right Rev. the Bishop of Oxford.
Abridged, in one volume Foolscap 8vo. With Portrait Price 6s in cloth

THE LIFE OF REV. ROWLAND HILL, M.A.
By the Rev. EDWIN SIDNEY, A M.
Fourth Edition. In foolscap, 8vo. Price 6s. in cloth.

A MEMOIR OF MISS MARY JANE GRAHAM,
Late of Stoke Fleming, Devon.
By the Rev. C. BRIDGES, Vicar of Old Newton, Suffolk.
Seventh Edition. In foolscap 8vo. With Portrait. Price 6s. in cloth.

MEMOIRS OF THE LIFE AND WRITINGS OF CLAUDIUS BUCHANAN, D.D.
By HUGH PEARSON, D.D, Dean of Salisbury.
With Portrait. Fourth Edition. Foolscap 8vo. Price 6s. in cloth

THE LIFE OF THE REV. THOMAS SCOTT,
Including a Narrative drawn up by himself, and copious extracts from his Correspondence.
With a Portrait. Ninth Edition. Foolscap 8vo. Price 6s. in cloth.

LIFE AND REMAINS OF THE REV. RICHARD CECIL, M.A.
By the Rev. JOSIAH PRATT, B.D.
Twelfth Edition, foolscap. Price 5s. cloth.

DOMESTIC PORTRAITURE:
Or, the successful application of Religious Principle in the Education of a Family, exemplified in the Memoirs of Three of the deceased Children of the Rev. LEGH RICHMOND,
Seventh Edition. Foolscap 8vo. With Engravings. Price 6s. in cloth

MEMORIALS OF TWO SISTERS.
By the Author of "Aids to Developement,' &c.
Fourth Edition. Corrected and considerably enlarged.
Foolscap 8vo. Price 5s. in cloth.

THE LIFE OF WILLIAM BEDELL, D.D.
LORD BISHOP OF KILMORE.
BY H. J. MONCK MASON, L.L.D; M R.I. A.
One Vol. 8vo. 10s. 6d. in cloth.

A MEMOIR OF MRS. WEST,

Wife of the Rev. J. West, of Chettle, Dorset.
Second Edition. With Vignette. In One Volume, crown octavo
Price 6s. cloth.

LETTERS AND PAPERS OF THE LATE
VISCOUNTESS POWERSCOURT.

Edited by the Rev. ROBERT DALY, A M. Rector of Powerscourt
Fifth Edition. In foolscap 8vo. Price 5s. in cloth

MEMOIRS OF THE REV. JOHN NEWTON,

Formerly Rector of St. Mary Woolnoth. With Selections from his
Correspondence. A new Edition, with Portrait and Engravings
Foolscap 8vo. Price 5s. in cloth.

THE LIFE OF THE REV. E. PAYSON, D.D.

Late Pastor of the Second Church in Portland, United States
Revised by the Rev. E. BICKERSTETH.
Third Edition. In foolscap. Price 5s. in cloth.

THE
LIFE OF AUGUSTUS HERMAN FRANKE,

Professor of Divinity, and Founder of the Orphan House at Halle
Translated from the German of Guericke.
By SAMUEL JACKSON.
With a Preface, by the Rev. E BICKERSTETH
Foolscap 8vo. With a Portrait. Price 5s. in cloth

THE
LIFE OF THE REV. DAVID BRAINERD,

Compiled from the Memoir by President EDWARDS
By the Rev JOSIAH PRATT, B D.
Foolscap 8vo. Price 5s. in cloth

MEMOIR AND REMAINS OF THE
REV. HENRY VAUGHAN, B.A.

Late of Worcester College, Oxford ; Vicar of Crickhowel, Brecknockshire,
and Minister of Park Chapel, Chelsea
One Vol. 12mo. Price 7s. 6d.

Practical and Devotional Works.

CHRISTIAN TRUTH;

A Family Guide to the Chief Truths of the Gospel; with Forms of prayer for each Day in the Week, and Private Devotions for various Occasions By the Rev. E. BICKERSTETH, Rector of Watton, Herts
Third Edition. in foolscap 8vo. price 6s. in cloth

BY THE SAME AUTHOR.

THE CHRISTIAN STUDENT;

Designed to assist Christians in general in acquiring Religious Knowledge With Lists of Books adapted to the various Classes of Society.
Fourth Edition. in foolscap 8vo. price 7s. cloth.

II.

A SCRIPTURE HELP;

Designed to assist in Reading the Bible profitably.
Nineteenth Edition, corrected and enlarged, With Maps.
in foolscap 8vo. price 5s. cloth.

III.

A TREATISE ON PRAYER;

Designed to promote the Spirit of Devotion.
Sixteenth Edition, corrected and enlarged. in foolscap 8vo price 5s. in cloth.

IV.

A TREATISE ON THE LORD'S SUPPER.

in Two parts.
Twelfth Edition. Foolscap. price 5s in cloth

V.

PRACTICAL

REFLECTIONS ON THE FOUR GOSPELS.

Arranged on the plan of a Harmony.
Which leaves each Gospel in the Distinct and Original Form
Selected from various Expositions
Second Edition. in foolscap 8vo. Price 5s. in cloth.

VI.

FAMILY EXPOSITIONS OF THE EPISTLES OF ST. JOHN AND ST. JUDE.

In foolscap 8vo. Price 3s. 6d. cloth.

THE CHRISTIAN MOURNER;

Select Passages from various Authors Edited by Mrs. DRUMMOND
With a Preface by the Rev. D.K. DRUMMOND, B A.
Minister of Trinity Chapel, Edinburgh
In foolscap 8vo. Price 5s. in cloth.

AN EXPOSITION OF PSALM CXIX:

as Illustrative of the Character of Christian Experience
By the Rev. C. BRIDGES, M.A., Vicar of Old Newton, Suffolk
In 12mo. Eighteenth Edition price 7s in cloth

BY THE SAME AUTHOR.

AN EXPOSITION OF THE BOOK OF PROVERBS.

Second Edition In two volumes. 12mo. Price 12s cloth

AN ESSAY ON FAMILY WORSHIP.

In Foolscap 8vo, Price 2s. cloth

CHRISTIAN RETIREMENT:

Or, Spiritual Exercises of the Heart
Thirteenth Edition, 12mo. price 6s. 6d. cloth.

JONAH'S PORTRAIT:

or, various Views of Human Nature, and of God's gracious Dealings
with Man in a fallen State. By the Rev. THOMAS JONES, Rector of Creaton
Eighth Edition. 16mo. price 3s 6d in cloth.

BY THE SAME AUTHOR.

THE PRODIGAL'S PILGRIMAGE

Into a far Country and back to his Father's House : in Fourteen Stages
Fourth Edition. in 16mo. price 3s 6d. in cloth.

II.

THE SCRIPTURE DIRECTORY;

or, an attempt to assist the Unlearned Reader to understand the
General History and Leading Subjects of the Bible
Eighth Edition. 12mo. price 5s. cloth.

THE CHRISTIAN'S MIRROR

of Duty to God and Man;
the Example of Christ illustrated from the Scriptures.
In 16mo. Price 2s. 6d. in cloth.

A BELIEVER'S MANUAL.

Containing the Points of a Christian's Experience.
By the Rev. JAMES MARRYAT, B A.
In 16mo. Price 3s. 6d. in cloth.

THE GREAT COMMANDMENT.

By the Author of "The Listener."
In foolscap octavo. Price 6s. in cloth.

BY THE SAME AUTHOR.

SUNDAY AFTERNOONS AT HOME.

In one vol. foolscap 8vo. Price 6s. cloth.

II.

CHRIST OUR LAW.

In One Volume. Foolscap 8vo. Price 6s. in cloth.

III.

THE TABLE OF THE LORD.

Second Edition. In foolscap 8vo. Price 4s. 6d. in cloth.

IV.

GATHERINGS.

In foolscap 8vo. Price 4s. 6d in cloth.

THE LAST DISCOURSE AND PRAYER

OF OUR LORD JESUS CHRIST WITH HIS DISCIPLES.
John xiii—xvii, with Practical Remarks
By the Rev. W. JOWETT, M.A.
In foolscap 8vo. Price 3s. 6d. in cloth.

BY THE SAME AUTHOR.

HELPS TO PASTORAL VISITATION:

In foolscap 8vo. Price 5s. in cloth

By Charlotte Elizabeth.

THE WAR WITH THE SAINTS.
In foolscap 8vo. *(In the Press)*

II.
JUDAH'S LION.
In foolscap 8vo. with Vignette. Third Edition Price 6s in cloth.

III.
CHAPTERS ON FLOWERS.
With Frontispiece, and twenty-seven Engravings. Fifth Edition.
In foolscap 8vo. Price 6s. in cloth

IV.
GLIMPSES OF THE PAST;
Being a continuation of "CHAPTERS ON FLOWERS"
Third Edition. With frontispiece, and numerous Engravings
In foolscap 8vo. Price 6s. in cloth.

V.
HELEN FLEETWOOD :
A Tale of the Factories.
With a Frontispiece, in foolscap octavo. Price 6s in cloth.

VI.
ENGLISH MARTYROLOGY :
From JOHN FOXE.
Two vols. with woodcuts. Price 12s in cloth

VII.
THE CHURCH VISIBLE IN ALL AGES.
In 16mo, with engravings. Price 3s. 6d. in cloth.

VIII.
PERSONAL RECOLLECTIONS.
In foolscap octavo, with Vignette. Price 6s. in cloth.

IX.
DANGERS AND DUTIES.
A Tale.
18mo. Price 2s. cloth.

X.
POSTHUMOUS AND OTHER POEMS.
In foolscap octavo. Price 5s. cloth

THE DAWN OF LIFE:

OR SCRIPTURE CONVERSIONS. BY A CLERGYMAN.
In one volume, foolscap, 8vo. price 3s. 6d. cloth.

PASSAGES FROM THE

LIFE OF A DAUGHTER AT HOME.

Third Edition. price 3s. 6d. cloth.

REDEMPTION IN ISRAEL.

Narratives of the lives of Converted Israelites,
By M. A. BARBER.
In foolscap 8vo. price 6s. in cloth.

MINUTIÆ;

or, Little Things for Christ's Flock.
365 daily Meditations on Scriptural Subjects.
By the Rev. J. W. PEERS, LL.D. Rector of Morden, Surrey.
Third Edition, much enlarged from the Author's Manuscripts.
12mo. price 5s. cloth.

A HISTORY OF THE JEWS,

From the Call of Abraham to the present time.
By the Rev. J .W. BROOKS, Vicar of Nottingham.
In foolscap octavo. price 6s. in cloth.

THE HOLY LAND:

BEING SKETCHES OF THE JEWS AND OF THE LAND OF PALESTINE.
With Engravings. In one Vol. foolscap. price 6s. cloth.

THE PILGRIM'S PROGRESS,

By JOHN BUNYAN.
With original notes by the late Rev. THOMAS SCOTT,
Illustrated with seventeen Engravings from the original designs
by the late T. STOTHARD, ESQ. R.A.
And twenty Woodcuts by S. WILLIAMS.
Price 1l 1s. in cloth, or 1l. 11s. 6d. in morocco, or with proofs on india
paper 1l 11s. 6d. in cloth, or 1l. 16s. half bound in morocco, gilt top.

LECTURES ON THE PILGRIM'S PROGRESS.

By the REV. C. OVERTON,
In 12mo. Price 3s.

THE
PORTRAITURE OF A CHRISTIAN LADY.
In foolscap 8vo. Price 4s. 6d. cloth.

THE PRACTICAL ASTRONOMER.
By Thomas Dick, L.L.D.
In one volume 12mo. With Engravings. price 10s. 6d. cloth

THE CHILD'S FIRST NOUN BOOK.
In square 16mo. price 1s.

DISTINCTION: A TALE.
By the Author of the "Baroness."
In two volumes, post octavo. price 16s. cloth.

THE DAYS OF LAUD;
And of the Commonwealth. A Narrative.
In 16mo. With Engravings. Price 4s. 6d. cloth.

HARMONIES OF SCRIPTURE;
and Short Lessons for young Children, with forty eight illustrations by Mr. Frank Howard. Arranged by J. D. Paul, Esq
In square 16mo. price 5s. boards.

STORIES OF THE PRIMITIVE AND EARLY CHURCH.
By Sophia Woodrooffe.
Edited by G.S. Faber, B.D.
Master of Sherburn Hospital and Prebendary of Salisbury
In 16mo. Price 3s. 6d. in cloth.

SKETCHES FOR YOUTH.
By Cæsar Malan, D.D.
In one volume 16mo. With Engravings. price 4s. 6d cloth.

MARY SPENCER.
A Tale for the Times. By Miss Howard
In 16mo. price 3s. 6d. cloth.

THE FEMALE VISITOR TO THE POOR.
By A Clergyman's Daughter.
In foolscap 8vo. Price 4s. 6d. cloth.

FELIX DE LISLE.
A Tale,
By Anne Flinders. Author of "Confessions of an Apostate," &c.
With a Frontispiece. price 3s. 6d. in cloth.

THE
HISTORY OF THE CHURCH OF CHRIST
From the Apostolical Times to the Rise of the Papal Apostasy.
Abridged from the work of the Rev. Joseph Milner, M A.
In One Vol. Foolscap 8vo. price 6s. in cloth.

THE
CHURCH OF CHRIST IN THE MIDDLE AGES.
By the Author of "Essays on the Church."
In One Vol. Foolscap 8vo. price 6s. in cloth

THE SCHOOL-GIRL IN FRANCE:
A Narrative addressed to Christian Parents.
Third Edition. In foolscap 8vo. With an engraved Title page.
price 5s. in cloth.

ROBERT AND FREDERICK:
A Boy's Book.
In foolscap octavo, with twenty Engravings. price 7s. in cloth.

AGATHOS: and OTHER SUNDAY STORIES,
By Samuel Wilberforce, M.A., Archdeacon of Surrey.
Sixth Edition. In 18mo. With Engravings. price 2s 6d. in cloth.

A KEY TO THE PRAYER BOOK,
OR AN ACCOUNT OF THE PRINCIPAL FORMULARIES OF
THE CHURCH OF ENGLAND.
By the Rev. Robert Whitehead, M.A
In one Vol. Foolscap 8vo. Price 6s. in cloth

THE NURSERY GOVERNESS.
By the Author of "The Week"
In 16mo. With Engravings. price 3s 6d in cloth.

BY THE SAME AUTHOR.
THE WEEK:
The Practical Duties of the Fourth Commandment Illustrated.
Royal 32mo. With Engravings Price 2s. 6d. cloth.
Or in Three parts. price 8d. each sewed.

II.
THE GUILTY TONGUE.
Royal 32mo. With Engravings. price 2s. 6d cloth.

III.
MEMORY'S RECORDS:
SHORT NARRATIVES FROM REAL LIFE.
Royal 32mo. With Engravings. price 2s 6d. cloth

IV.
THE HOUSE OF THE THIEF;
Or, the Eighth Commandment practically Illustrated.
in Royal 32mo. With Engravings. price 2s. 6d. cloth

V.
MY STATION AND ITS DUTIES
A Narrative for Girls going to Service.
Royal 32mo. With Engravings. price 2s 6d. cloth.

VI.
GOING TO SERVICE.
A Sequel to "My Station and its Duties."
Royal 32mo. With Engravings. price 2s. 6d. cloth

VII.
THE COMMANDMENT WITH PROMISE.
Royal 32mo. With Engravings. price 2s 6d. cloth.

VIII.
TRACTS:
Containing THE DARK, THE RAINBOW, THE SUNBEAM,
NOT ALONE, THE WITNESS.
price 2s. 6d. half-bound.

IX.
INSTRUCTIVE FABLES FOR CHRISTIAN SCHOLARS.
18mo, with engravings. price 1s. 6d. cloth.

THE BREAD OF DECEIT:
Illustrated in the History of Maurice Chalmers.
Fifth Edition. Royal 32mo. With Engravings. price 2s. 6d. cloth.

BY THE SAME AUTHOR.

CHRISTIAN TRIALS.
A NARRATIVE DRAWN FROM REAL LIFE.
In 18mo. With Frontispiece. price 2s. 6d. half-bound

II.
THE FIRST LENT LILIES;
Second Edition, with a Frontispiece.
In 18mo. Price 6d. sewed.

III.
THE DEBTOR:
A Narrative from Real Life.
price 4d.

THE NEW COMMANDMENT;
Or, the Christian's Test.
With two Woodcuts. price 2s. 6d. cloth.

MARY ATKINS:
Or, Nature and Grace.
"If any man be in Christ, he is a new creature."
18mo. price 1s. cloth.

SOMETHING ELSE.
"One thing is needful." By MIRIAM.
18mo. price 6d. sewed.

BUNYAN'S PILGRIM'S PROGRESS.
A new Edition, with 27 Woodcuts. Small 8vo. Price 4s. cloth.

SABBATH MUSINGS AND EVERY DAY SCENES.

In foolscap 8vo. price 6s. in cloth

BY THE SAME AUTHOR.

THE LOST FARM;

Or, the Effects of a Lie. Second Edition.
18mo. price 6d. sewed.

II.

THE VISIT TO CLARINA;

Or, the Effects of Revenge.
18mo. price 2s. cloth.

III.

THE HAPPY FAMILY;

Or, Talents Well-Employed. Second Edition
18mo. price 6d sewed.

SCRIPTURE BIOGRAPHY FOR THE YOUNG

with Critical Illustrations and Practical Remarks
JUDGES. RUTH.
By the Rev. T. H GALLAUDET.
With Twelve Woodcuts. price 3s. cloth

BIBLE STORIES FOR THE YOUNG,

with Critical Illustrations and Practical Remarks
ADAM TO JACOB.
By the Rev. T. H. GALLAUDET
With Frontispiece. price 2s 6d. cloth

THE NUN:

A NARRATIVE. With Engravings
Fifth Edition. In 16mo. price 5s. in cloth.

LITTLE MARY;

Or, God in Every Thing. Two Parts. 18mo. Price 1s. 6d.

YOUTHFUL PIETY EXEMPLIFIED

In the last Illness and Death of Ann Clitheroe.
By the Rev. J. COTTERILL, Rector of Blakeney, Norfolk.
18mo. price 1s. 6d. cloth.

SUNDAY EVENING INSTRUCTION,

or the Catechism of the Church of England explained,
By a CLERGYMAN'S WIFE.
16mo. Price 3s. 6d. cloth.

EMILY;

Or, Recollections of a Wayward Child.
By L. L.
Second Edition. Price 6d.

THE PASTOR'S DAUGHTER:

Or, Conversations between the late Dr. Payson and his Child, on the way of Salvation by Jesus Christ.
Third Edition, Enlarged. Price 2s. cloth.

ELIZABETH ALLEN,

or the Faithful Servant. By the Author of "SOPHIA DE LISSAU."
In 18mo. Price 2s 6d. half-bound.

THE HAPPY MUTE;

Or, the Dumb Child's Appeal.
By CHARLOTTE ELIZABETH.
Seventh Edition. 18mo. Price 6d.

THE TWO KINGDOMS.

An Allegory,
In 18mo. Price 2s. in cloth.

PARTING WORDS.

ADDRESSED TO THE CONGREGATION OF TRINITY CHURCH, MARGATE.

May 24, 1846. By their late Minister the Rev. J STREATFIELD, M.A
Incumbent of Uckfield, Sussex.
In 18mo. Price 1s. 6d. cloth.

SCRIPTURE INSTRUCTION FOR THE LEAST AND THE LOWEST.

In Three Volumes, 18mo. Second Edition. Price 10s. 6d cloth.

AGNES MORTON:
OR, THE IDOLATRY OF THE HEART.

By the Author of the "BREAD OF DECEIT"
In eighteens   Price 2s. 6d.

A BOOK FOR THE COTTAGE,
OR, THE HISTORY OF MARY AND HER FAMILY.

In eighteens   Price 2s 6d.

DAILY BREAD,
OR, A TEXT OF SCRIPTURE CONTAINING A DUTY AND A PROMISE FOR EVERY DAY IN THE YEAR.

Selected by a LADY,
with a morning and evening prayer for every day in the week
18mo. 6d. sewed; or 1s in cloth.

THE BLESSING OF PEACE,

By the Author of "a Visit to my Birth Place."
32mo. price 1s cloth.

A HELP FOR THE WEARY CHRISTIAN,

Third Edition. 18mo. Price 6d. gilt edges.

THE TWO BUCKETS;

Or, the Power of prayer.
Second Edition.   Price 4d.

GEORGE STANLEY.

"In due season ye shall reap, if ye faint not."
Third Edition.   price 2d.

HUMBLING RECOLLECTIONS OF MY MINISTRY.
By a Clergyman.
Second edition. Price 6d.

REASONS FOR GOING TO CHURCH.
Price 3d.

THINK BEFORE YOU SPEAK.
Price 3d.

HEADS OF PRAYER FOR DAILY PRIVATE DEVOTION;
with an Appendix of occasional prayers 18mo. Price 6d

THOUGHTS ON CONVERSION;
in nine letters, addressed to a young relation. 18mo. Price 1s.

THE COTTAGER'S DICTIONARY OF THE BIBLE,
in which the meaning of every important word is explained.
By the Rev. J. K. Whish, M.A.
Revised by the Rev. C. H. Lutwidge, M A.
18mo Price 1s. in cloth.

RIGHT THOUGHTS IN SAD HOURS.
By Cotton Mather, D.D. 32mo. Price 1s.

SCRIPTURE OUTLINES;
a Course of Religious Instruction for the Sunday School or the Family
By the Rev. J. M. Randall. Curate of Lowestoft.
Third Edition, 12mo. 9d. sewed.

Uniform with the above, price 6d.
PART 1 OF THE SECOND SERIES OF
SCRIPTURE OUTLINES;
Comprising an arrangement of Sunday Lessons on the Epistles and Gospels, from Advent Sunday to Trinity Sunday.